Praise for *Elder Care Made Easier*

The families who care for seniors face a variety of challenges. The complex care for an aging loved on is no longer a task suitable for the uninformed adult child. The practical tips and resources provided by Dr. Marion Somers are clearly articulated and sourced with the non-professional caregiver in mind. Dr. Somers' deep understanding of caregiving trends and breadth of experience in senior care make *Elder Care Made Easier* a must-read for anyone who wants to avoid a health care crisis.

—Tafa Jefferson
Founder, Amada Senior Care

Anyone at any age should have this book at the ready. I've always recommended this book to my clients and now I'm using it for my mother and myself as we age together. Thanks Dr. Marion for bringing sensible, organized planning to our lives.

—DorothytheOrganizer,
America's Most Innovative Organizer and Expert,
Host on the Emmy-nominated hit TV show *Hoarders*

I am thoroughly impressed with the practical insights offered by Doctor Marion in this excellent book.

—Debbie Bitticks
Intergenerational Expert, Award Winning Author, Health and Caregiving Advocate, Co-founder/Co-creator Digital Life Cloud

Dr. Marion Somers' book is an important guide to caregivers who continually face challenges. We have an ever-increasing number of elders needing assistance from caregivers who are without special training, financial resources, and advisors. This book fills a great need to giving counsel to them.

—Andrew Kluger
Managing Partner
Bluegrass Assisted Living Properties

Elder Care Made Easier.

Doctor*Marion's* 10 Steps
to Help You Care for an
Aging Loved One

Second Edition

Marion Somers, Ph.D.

Patty Strahl's sister

Addicus Books
Omaha, Nebraska

An Addicus Nonfiction Book

ISBN: 978-1-950091-20-1

Cover design by Peri Poloni-Gabriel

Typography by Jack Kusler

This book is not intended to serve as a substitute for a physician. Nor is the author's intention to give medical advice contrary to that of an attending physician.

Library of Congress Cataloging-in-Publication Data

Names: Somers, Marion, – author.
Title: Elder care made easier : Doctor Marion's 10 steps to help you care for an aging loved one / Marion Somers, Ph.D.
Description: Second edition. | Omaha, Nebraska : Addicus Books, [2020] | "An Addicus Nonfiction Book." | Identifiers: LCCN 2020024073 (print) | LCCN 2020024074 (e-book) | ISBN 9781950091201 (trade paperback) | ISBN 9781950091218 (pdf) | ISBN 9781950091232 (kindle edition) | ISBN 9781950091225 (e-pub)
Subjects: LCSH: Older people—Care. | Frail elderly—Care. | Caregivers.
Classification: LCC HV1451 .S64 2020 (print) | LCC HV1451 (ebook) | DDC
649.8084/6—dc23
LC record available at https://lccn.loc.gov/2020024073
LC ebook record available at https://lccn.loc.gov/2020024074

Addicus Books, Inc.
P.O. Box 45327
Omaha, Nebraska 68145
AddicusBooks.com
Printed in the United States of America
10 9 8 7 6 5 4 3 2 1

To Craig M. Caryl, a man with big ideas who always carries them through to completion, and to Marc Matthew Harris, the younger brother I never had.

Contents

Acknowledgments

To Sandra Colette Caryl, who was a constant sounding board throughout the writing process, thank you for helping me probe deeper to access the most vital stories and information, and for simplifying things so that the material is easier for the reader to understand and utilize.

To Kesiah E. Scully, a friend with deep devotion to my growth as a creative person. Thank you for faithfully reading everything I've ever written. Thank you to Cary T. Kellems, Donald Hugh, Corina Gheorghiu and Grig Gheorghiu, Lynne Caryl, Pam Solberg-Tapper, Ruth Baumann, Cortney Kluger, Galina Kovahilasky, Dr. Damien F. Goldberg, Dr. Alan Kaplan, Christie Dungey, and Edgar H Coxeter.

My love and gratitude go out to my family, both in the United States and in Toronto, Canada, who have supported my writing efforts.

Finally, I wish to heartily embrace all of the elderly who have come into my life and blessed me in countless ways. You have shown me how to live each day fully and how to stay in the now of each moment. You have taught me to count my blessings on a daily basis. I have accumulated many memories and stories and good times in your company. I now try to enjoy life and meet each occasion with the openness, humility, and humor that so many of you have shown me.

Foreword

I am an entrepreneur who did very well at the crossroads of taxation and technology and, although it pains me to admit, I'm getting old. There is no denying it and, frankly, avoiding it really isn't an option. I never saw my parents age—they both passed relatively young—but my own son and daughter have courtside seats to my advancing years. Still for now, I am a spry octogenarian who cycles sixty miles a week, who holds my own at the bridge table, and started my latest and most exciting business venture at age seventy-nine.

And that's where my friendship with Dr. Marion began. The American population is aging and with that process comes the decline of our bodily functions, and yes, I am referring to incontinence. It's an unpleasant reality in store for many of us. With Dr. Marion's help, our business created an absorbent product for male incontinence that changes out effortlessly and is easy on both patients and caregivers. Through our many hours together designing, redesigning, and testing the product, Dr. Marion has given me a glimpse into the complexities families face in caring for their aging loved ones.

I have seen Dr. Marion shepherd her often bewildered clients through the labyrinth of our elder care system. She is a brilliant and tireless champion for our seniors who helps each client devise the best solution to their unique predicament. I am grateful she has taken the time to put her wisdom into print so that my own children have a reliable resource to consult when the time comes for them to look after me.

If you've cracked the spine of this book, I suspect you are facing the challenges of caring for your own aging parent, relative or friend. Maybe you are not a procrastinator and purchased this book long before you need it, but I doubt it. An emergency is looming, or has already come, and now you're desperate for reliable information to make quick decisions. Don't worry, you are in good hands. Dr. Marion draws on her decades as an elder care manager to outline what's in store for you, what resources you can draw on, and how to make this time with your elder less burdensome and more meaningful for you both.

Good luck.

J. Baum Harris,
Chairman and Managing Director,
UI Medical

Preface

Many refer to our era as "the aging of America." It's true that our elders represent a significant and growing segment of the population. More families are faced with the challenges of caring for an elderly relative or friend than ever before. This is a role reversal in many cases. The parent or elder relative requires care and the adult child becomes the caregiver. The caregiver must make choices for the elder that affect not only the parent but often the entire family. There's a tremendous need for information about health care and financial, housing, and legal issues, to name just a few. Elder care issues are constantly changing, and people need guidance on how to facilitate access to the many benefits available. It can be a daunting task to make these decisions, and it can make a caregiver feel overwhelmed.

A recurring question I hear as an advocate for seniors is whether there is a guide book or "road map" to help caregivers navigate this confusing elder care maze. Doctor Marion has provided just such a book. *Elder Care Made Easier* is an invaluable elder care resource that also provides a healthy dose of hope in Doctor Marion's trademark warm manner. For many caregivers, this is a new journey, one filled with uncertainty and obstacles. It's often the first time in their lives that they've had to care for an aging relative or friend. *Elder Care Made Easier* provides the tools to help caregivers make educated and thoughtful decisions as they face the many challenges ahead.

For many years, I've had the privilege of meeting thousands of people who struggle to care for their elderly relatives and friends in the most dignified and compassionate manner. The good news is that due to advances in modern medicine, seniors are living longer. But the bad news is that many seniors are outliving their resources. They're unable to pay for the items necessary to maintain the quality of life they've enjoyed in the past. Caregivers are left with the task of finding alternative ways to provide for their care and comfort. *Elder Care Made Easier* is filled with guidance that will improve the quality of an elder's life as well as the life of the caregiver.

Many families embark on this journey of caring for an aging relative unaware of how to pay for the cost of long-term care. They have no plan of action for the future and are faced with decisions they're unprepared to make. In her book, Doctor Marion outlines specific solutions and options that families can explore when considering how to provide for care. *Elder Care Made Easier* provides a wealth of information and resources to assist a caregiver in overcoming the many barriers that exist. After reading this book, caregivers will have a frame of reference to guide the many choices they'll need to consider. This book also provides comfort and support. And very important, it also validates feelings and helps caregivers move forward with a workable plan in place for the future.

Seniors and their caregivers need to recognize the need for advanced long-term planning and organization. This book provides guidance in an efficient, easy-to-understand manner. The "10 steps" format answers most elder care questions and points caregivers in the right direction so that they will feel less besieged. Doctor Marion's book also includes several templates to organize information pertaining to a senior's health, legal situation, finances, and lifestyle. The Sample Skill Inventory is especially useful for caregivers as they try to better understand exactly what kind of mental, physical, and psychological shape their elder loved one is in.

The need for Doctor Marion's book is also great due to a change in our political climate. Our federal, state, and local governments are under increasing fiscal constraints, and health care is the single fastest-growing component of many government budgets. Even though seniors represent a growing political presence, there is enormous pressure to cut costs for their care. Congress recently passed legislation that will have a dramatic effect on seniors' ability to access government benefits for long-term care. More changes are sure to follow at the state and local levels. Access to prescription drug plans and long-term care insurance continues to cause concern among our elders. Many don't understand the options available, so the need for guidance in these areas has never been greater. Fortunately, Doctor Marion provides a comprehensive resource section that's filled with links to information that will keep both caregivers and the elderly current.

Society is finally recognizing that we must honor our elders. The wisdom and guidance that they provide to subsequent generations is priceless. As Doctor Marion observes, "They have earned their wrinkles." I have known Doctor Marion for many years, and she continues to be an inspirational and powerful voice for our elderly population. In her book she also shows us how to preserve and appreciate their wisdom. Every person who takes on the role of caregiver should read *Elder Care Made Easier* and be comforted by the knowledge contained within. It's a straightforward and often heart-warming read that serves as an unrivaled source of guidance for the often challenging but equally rewarding journey of elder care.

— Bernard A. Krooks,
Certified Elder Law Attorney
President, New York Chapter of the
National Academy of Elder Law Attorneys

Introduction

The aging of the American population is a relatively new phenomenon caused by the confluence of health care improvements, pharmaceutical innovations, healthier lifestyle choices, and the sheer mass of the Baby Boomer generation. The oldest Baby Boomers (those born 1946–1964) turned sixty in 2006. They were the first wave of a looming elder care crisis.

Chances are, you picked up this book because you have an elder parent, spouse, or loved one who is in declining health, and you've become the primary caregiver. I understand that you feel scared, overworked, and underappreciated. My goal is to provide a book that gives you answers and direction to help you cope with your new caregiving role.

I'm Doctor Marion Somers, a geriatric care manager. Boy, do I know what you are going through. You know something must be done to take care of your elder loved one, and you are feeling overwhelmed. I want to remind you that you're not alone. Relax, take a deep breath, and let's begin your caregiving journey together.

Over many years of providing care for more than 3,000 clients, I've learned a thing or two about elder care. In this book, I share my wisdom and techniques in a concise 10-step plan geared for everyday individuals. You can read all 10 steps as an entire elder care program, or you can focus directly on the step (or steps) most relevant to your elder's current situation. Most of my clients require the majority of my 10 steps, but I want you to use only what you feel comfortable with. Focus on what can be achieved both in the near term and in the long term.

Chances are you're not a trained caregiver, and the last thing you want to do is wade through complicated information at this difficult time. That's why I wrote this book—to save you time, money, and heartache; to show you how to become a skilled caregiver; to cheer you on through your difficult task; and, most important, to give you hope in your time of need.

As a youngster, I discovered I had a natural rapport with senior citizens. I used to get groceries for the elderly who lived in my East Harlem neighborhood. Those encounters gave me some spending money but, more importantly, made me understand that the elderly matter in society. I don't focus on their grey hair or wrinkles. Instead, I'm inspired by the depth, breadth, and beauty of their life experiences—and you should be, too. If someone has lived to be ninety years old, he or she must have some life skills and street smarts to make sure vital needs get met. It's crucial that we tap into the wisdom, strength, life strategies, and stories of the elderly before they pass on. I wish that as a culture we were more prepared to care for the elderly. I hope this book helps you do just that.

I want to spread a message of healing, hope, and life to as many people as I can. Other elder care books can be too impersonal, too focused on one aspect of the process, too dense and filled with details that can bog you down, or not practical enough in their approach. My goal was to come up with an executable elder care plan that's written in plain language. I want to make this traditionally difficult subject as accessible as possible. You don't need a vast knowledge of medical terminology. What you must possess is a strong desire to see things through. Giving care to an elder loved one may not be easy, but it can be a rewarding experience.

I've made caring for the elderly my life's work. I think of myself as a compass that gives my clients the directions they need to navigate the stormy elder care seas. The elderly and their caregivers benefit from my experience, knowledge, and know-how. And now, so will you. But by no means am I a miracle worker. For any of my proven steps to work, you must put in the time and effort required to benefit your elder.

Millions of Baby Boomers have spent recent years caring for their parents, and they'll soon require elder care, too. The U.S. Bureau of the Census estimates that from 2000 to 2030

Introduction

the number of sixty-five to seventy-four-year-old Americans will increase by a staggering 75 percent. The emotional and financial toll for families facing elder care can be crippling, which makes this the biggest challenge for the American social system in the decades ahead.

Just by reading this far, you're light-years ahead of most individuals. All the same, you may be feeling overwhelmed by a combination of anxiety, sadness, guilt, anger, hurt, fear, stress, frustration, and loneliness. But you're not trapped! My 10-step plan can help alleviate today's crisis. It allows you to free up your thoughts and energies so that you can focus on more fulfilling moments with your elder loved one. This approach will save you time, money, and especially emotional stress. The 10 steps can even turn your caregiving challenge into the role of a lifetime.

At the same time, it's crucial that you remember to take care of yourself. In all likelihood, you have suddenly been thrust into the role of caregiver. Last month, your elder was perfectly fine over the phone, but then an episode (a fall, a stroke, a heart attack, memory failure, confusion) occurred, and it seems as if things are spiraling out of control. Even if you've become a caregiver gradually, you're still not professionally, mentally, or emotionally prepared for it. It's important to approach the task in an organized manner, or you may soon see your own family life and professional life begin to slip away. My 10-step approach will get you organized and help you avoid a state of chaos.

Much of the information will seem like common sense once you've read it, and guess what—you're right! It is common sense that has been crystallized to its essence during my thirty years of dealing with elder care issues, clients, and dilemmas. You have to become a detective and discover the truth about your loved one's medications, safety, finances, legal situations, and so on. A lot of information is required in order for you to have a comprehensive understanding of what needs to be done to manage your elder's condition. That is your new challenge.

I hope you're still at a time when something can be done to improve your elder's situation. Be proactive, not reactive, whenever possible. If you're in a reactive mode after a serious episode involving your elder, you've still come to the right place. Chances are you'll have to utilize more than one of the steps in this book right away. Take a deep breath and begin. I try to be a calm refuge for my clients every day. I'm like a cork on life's turbulent seas, staying afloat no matter how big a wave comes along. I'll hold your hand through difficult times and help you be proactive. I will also help you react to what has come your way by sharing practical knowledge that should improve the situation.

This is an action book. Based on the immediate need, I lay out what must be done and then set realistic, doable goals so that you can see your progress. You must attack the immediate problem areas first, and then prioritize the other steps along the way so that you can take care of them next week, next month, or even next year if possible.

Keep this book handy. You never know when you might need it, since caregiving challenges can occur at a moment's notice. You might not need to read the book in its entirety right now. Especially if you're in crisis mode, find the step that directly addresses your elder's immediate need. Then, when you have time, read the other steps. You'll likely need to follow all 10 steps by the time your caregiving journey comes to an end. Share the book with your relatives, too. So much of your responsibility will involve other family members. It's important to bring them into the loop, because the more they understand about the process, the more helpful they're likely to be, and the less overwhelmed and isolated you'll feel. These 10 steps are like the ten fingers on my two healing hands, reaching out to support you and your elder in a time of need and transition.

We usually receive more from our elders than we can ever give in return. Try to learn from your elder's wisdom and experience. I look forward to the day when we change the commonly assumed equations that say aging equals decline and youth equals perfection. The natural chain of events in life actually operates on the exact opposite premise. Caregivers must enjoy the windfall of their elders' knowledge. They are a valuable resource that needs to be appreciated. I hope each one of you finds this an enlightening, valuable approach to elder care. I find helping others to be very rewarding, and I hope this book can guide you on your caregiving journey. It could be the most rewarding challenge you ever undertake.

Step 1

Communicate Openly

*Improving communication in our family reduced my
mother's fears and enabled us to open up for the first time in
years. As soon as the in-fighting stopped, my family was able to
make better decisions for my mother's future.*
—A.C., California

The single most difficult challenge you face as a caregiver could be managing communication—with the
person you're caring for, your extended family, other professionals involved in your elder's situation, and, surprisingly,
even yourself. Honest, open, crystal clear communication
should be your goal. Why? Every time the lines of communication are unclear or broken off, your ability to make smart
decisions is hampered. You could have arguments with loved
ones, or expect the impossible from doctors, or cause your
elder to become irritated by a situation you thought you had
under control. Have the strength to implement a communication strategy that gets to the truth of your elder's situation.

Results of a recent study show that only 7 percent of all
spoken words are listened to. Thirty-eight percent of verbal
communication is understood by volume, pitch, and rhythm.
The remaining 55 percent is determined by body language and
facial expressions. Be aware of your tone, volume, delivery,
and body language when communicating with others.

The simplest part of communication, as well as the hardest
part, is listening. Early in my career I learned this lesson from
one of my most vocal clients, who also happened to be an

1

excellent listener. She had the ability to listen with her heart and soul to what was said. She would say that she also listened to what someone's body told her. When I asked her how she had become so skilled, she said, "We were given two eyes, two ears, and one mouth. If I listen and observe twice as much as I talk, I'll be able to understand not just what people are saying but also what they truly mean." I always try to listen twice as often as I speak.

Communicate with Your Elder

Your communication efforts should begin with a one-on-one discussion with your elder in order to figure out what issues need to be addressed. Start by building trust. Your elder has to know that you understand his or her values, struggles, and identity. When that happens, barriers disappear.

My clients often ask me, "Why is my mother so nice to you? She hasn't been that nice to us in years." I think it's because I don't judge my clients. I don't arrive with baggage from the past or preconceived notions of who my client is. I know this is difficult to do, but you should try, both for your sake and your elder's. Also, try to find the humor in any situation. Believe me, your elder is full of humor and wisdom. You don't have your needs met for decades without learning how to laugh and how to get what you want. Caregiving is a chance to embrace your elder emotionally and to work together to find answers and harmony.

As you listen and observe, focus on the *activities of daily living, or ADLs.* These are the activities of daily living a senior encounters. Your elder will require assistance with some ADLs, whereas other ADLs might still be easily managed. The sum of your elder's ability to manage ADLs will give you a clear picture of his or her real condition. Also, look closely for signs that your elder exhibits while mentally retrieving information. Each person has a unique way of retrieving details, and usually his or her eyes will seek out the same spot while doing it. But if people lie or are not fully functional on a mental level, they often look elsewhere to retrieve the answer. Also, their cheeks flush, and their palms get sweaty. Be aware of these visual signals so that you can pick up on your elder's mental ability.

Step 1: Communicate Openly

Thirty-eight percent of those sixty-five and over are diagnosed with a severe disability, and 47 percent of those eighty-five and over have Alzheimer's disease or another form of dementia.

To determine your elder's personal attentiveness, basic wellness, thought patterns, and speaking skills, get answers to the following thirty-nine questions (there may be others). Answers to these questions will give you a baseline from which you can plan to meet your caregiving challenges. It might seem surprising, but some people start the caregiving process without asking their elder even one question.

- Is he or she getting any exercise?
- Is he or she getting enough fresh air?
- Did he or she stop going to the barber shop (beauty parlor)?
- Does he or she have foul body odor?
- Is he or she wearing torn clothing?
- What is his or her sleep pattern?
- Can he or she drive without incident?
- Is his or her general hygiene suffering?
- Is his or her mail opened?
- Are his or her bills overdue?
- Is his or her checking account overdrawn?
- Has he or she lost all interest in money?
- Have his or her drug prescriptions not been filled or are they out of date?
- Does he or she avoid answering the phone or calling people back?
- Are plants in the house and in the garden dying?
- Is the lawn overgrown with weeds?
- Is his or her home a mess or in disrepair?
- Is trash everywhere?
- Is laundry everywhere?
- Does he or she have any unusual bruises or scratches?

- Is his or her eyesight diminished?
- Does he or she have a hearing loss?
- Has he or she been falling down or losing balance frequently?
- Is he or she wetting the bed or battling incontinence?
- Is he or she shunning friends and/or family?
- Has he or she lost interest in former passions or hobbies?
- Has he or she undergone a medical crisis or the loss of a loved one?
- Does he or she cry often or is he or she prone to fits of anger?
- Can he or she remember what he or she had for breakfast?
- Has he or she been experiencing short-term memory loss?
- Does he or she become easily confused, irrational, or upset?
- Does he or she wander away from the home or get lost?
- Does he or she frequently stammer and search for the correct word in conversation?
- Does he or she repeat conversation?
- Does he or she wear the same clothes?
- Is his or her personality inconsistent?
- Does he or she forget family members' names?
- Does he or she have a diminished sense of day, month, or year?
- Has he or she lost the sense of taste?

After you've gathered the answers, you'll be able to clearly understand problematic areas that require attention and care. The good news is that you should also be comforted by the ADLs your elder can still perform. Focus on them, since positive reinforcement and taking advantage of what still "works" can go a long way toward keeping your elder a vital part of the family and community.

Make Special Considerations

Sit where your elder would like you to. Don't violate personal space; ask, "Where would you like me to sit?" Include your elder in the decision-making process whenever possible. This is empowering. Sit in a well-lit room where there is good light on your face. Your elder might even be lip-reading and not be aware of it. Clean his or her eyeglasses if necessary. Take food with you so that there's a tasty treat every now and then, but be sure it meets all dietary requirements. Try not to be interrupted by phone calls, the computer, TV, radio, and visitors. Take care of the simple creature comforts. Have your elder sit in a favorite chair. If you don't make the simple effort, your elder's focus will be on personal needs that aren't being met, instead of on conversation.

Start with Chit Chat

Start all conversations with chit chat about your elder and the day. Tell your elder why you're there; don't ask if he or she knows why you're there. Always make your elder the center of attention. Be light, gentle, and general, and talk about the big events of the day. Don't focus on problems or specifics until you have to. Discuss familiar topics, not the latest top-selling rap album. Ask questions like "Tell me about your childhood, your children, your husband, or your wife." Keep your sentences short and concise. Ask questions and wait for the answers before rushing to the next subject. Give your elder time to process and formulate answers. Limit your vocabulary, stay on one subject, and say one sentence at a time. Be careful not to send mixed messages, and don't use slang or current vernacular that may not be understood. Ensure that what you're saying is accurate. If it's not true, don't say it. Do not exaggerate.

Tips for Holding Attention

Consider wearing bright clothing (red works best) and shiny jewelry to keep his or her attention on you. Make direct eye contact and let him or her get used to your scent; hold his or her hands and do anything you can think of to make a direct human connection. Don't begin every conversation by talking about his or her ailments. Instead, talk about positive memories and important people from his or her life. This talk can be triggered by an item found in the house such as an old photo, a piece of furniture, or a travel memento. If he or she is bedridden or in a wheelchair, make sure you communicate at eye level when possible. Being at a level higher than him or her is an unintentional power play that affects communication.

Paraphrase Often

Paraphrasing what your elder says lets him or her know that he or she has been heard and lets you know that you've been heard; it also allows you to provide clarifications. If conflicts arise, face them directly. This usually dissipates the problem. Get feedback from your elder, too. Ask things like "Can you be more specific about that?" Use positive reinforcement. This is all about making your elder feel good and establishing a rapport, which is especially challenging if you haven't had a good relationship in the past. Find something positive to relate that will increase your bond. Even if the only fond memory you have is of mom's chocolate chip cookies, let her know how much you loved them. Honor who she is and who she was.

Announce Your Visit

Let your elder know when you will be coming. Call ahead of time. Ring the doorbell or knock on the door before entering if your elder is in a nursing facility or hospital. You wouldn't like it if people barged into your home unannounced, even if they were taking care of you. Let him or her know why you're there—to cook a meal, to drive to the doctor, or to let the plumber in. Be polite and considerate. Respect space, both physical and emotional space, and never take it for granted.

Keep Seniors Involved

Aging can be a cruel process, and being removed from your family's communication loop can be most cruel of all. Your job as a caregiver is to limit his or her feelings of isolation and frustration. Show you care by visiting in person or over the phone. Send an e-mail message, a greeting card, or a handwritten note.

Step 1: Communicate Openly

A simple gesture can make someone feel wonderful. Contact them via Skype or FaceTime at a predetermined time regularly.

Many of your elder's choices are disappearing, so it's important that you involve him or her in every decision when possible. Does she want to wear the blue dress or the green dress? Does he or she want to drink apple juice or orange juice? Ask him or her what color bed linens or comforter cover he or she would like. Consider using flannel sheets in the winter since they're especially soft and warm.

Also, brighten your elder's day. It's important to have living things around. Bring colorful fresh flowers that smell good. Awaken the olfactory senses. Baby powder is a favorite, as are the aromas of ground coffee beans, orange peels, watermelons, and vials of lavender. Smells can trigger good memories that lead to hours of positive stories and feelings.

Discuss Finances

Although you may have never discussed these touchy subjects before, it's time to shed light on your elder's finances and legal situation. It might be difficult to discuss topics that have previously been off-limits, but it's crucial that you have this information. Imagine yourself in your elder's shoes. Consider the mental and physical situation, and then try to think of what you would like done and said for you, as well as what you'd like to remain private. *See* Step 5: Manage Financial Issues, and Step 6: Take Care of Legal Matters for more details regarding how to handle these extremely private topics.

Don't Focus on Past Conflicts

Be extra sensitive about how you bring up unresolved history. Bringing up such subjects can cause your elder to tune you out or become upset. What happened in the past happened then, and people have their own perspective of what occurred. Your elder can become entrenched, and that's no position to be in now. If something must be done about the past, encourage your elder to let go, but don't ever put him or her in a defensive position.

If your elder would like to face tough issues from the past with people who've passed on, suggest he or she close his or her eyes and then talk about it. This exercise can really help someone express repressed feelings. Your elder can reach a sense of finality this way, too. It's vital that your elder get rid of any accumulated baggage and unburden him or herself of old grudges, hurts, and heavy loads that could make it more painful to pass on from this earthly experience. By encouraging open communication, you can lead your elder down a path of positive reflection that wipes the slate clean before the end of the human journey.

I once had a client who was being taken care of by her three adult daughters. Each one of them individually told me how the mother had favored another sister, and each time it was a different sister. There was so much conflict that I told them to drop the nonsense from that moment forward. They did, and the final six months of their mother's life included many of her happiest days.

My personal experience has been, after being at the bedside of so many people as they make the transition from this life to whatever comes next, that those who are still holding on to anger, frustration, and the "would have, could have, should have," have a painful transition. Whereas those who have made peace and who have let go of all the negativity and are living in the now, have a much easier time transitioning.

Emotional Disclosure

Allow your elder's feelings to surface. Facilitate open, honest dialogue. Never try to suppress things he or she wants to discuss. This time is usually filled with reflection and new understanding, and your elder will probably want to talk to someone about it. That someone can be you. Validate emotions. Your elder might say, "I'm afraid of going to the hospital." Acknowledge the comment and agree that you understand how that could be disquieting. You might not ameliorate any fears, but at least your elder won't be alone with them any longer.

As many elderly come to the end of life, even those who say they don't believe in a higher power question what they've done with their lives. Believers and nonbelievers alike become more appreciative of the sunset, the stars, and a newborn baby. Allowing your elder to discuss his or her deepest thoughts is a vital part of caregiving. Your elder needs someone to talk to about their time on earth. It's often to address unresolved pain or anger that has been carried around, sometimes for decades. Doing so frees your elder to face the next journey, wherever that may be. Facilitating this conversation is important. Help your elder appreciate the small things in life and work through painful issues with you, another family member, or a therapist.

Stay Positive

Your elder might strike out at you verbally, but you have to stay positive. I once had a frail and usually quiet woman erupt suddenly. She said, "You're one nosy bitch!" I replied matter-of-factly, "Yes, I like to know a lot of things. I know a lot of things about you." From then on, she was much more communicative with me. Your elder wants to be heard. Pay respect and treat your elder as a vital member of the family. He or she is not a burden. Insist on adult-to-adult communication. Never talk down to your elder or treat him or her like a child. That only adds to the resentment and the feeling that others have taken over his or her life. Don't discuss your elder's ailments with others as if he or she isn't present. This also takes away your loved one's personal power.

Embrace Technology

During your elder's lifetime, the way we communicate has changed at warp speed. Your elder may not be comfortable with recent technological advances, and it's your task to teach him or her. I highly recommend you make sure he or she is comfortable using a computer. Show how to log on and log off, and how to access the Internet and e-mail. Write it out step by step and go over the instructions in person. Turn any fear of the computer into an opportunity to bond. Using e-mail and texting can change your elder's life because staying in touch with younger relatives (especially grandchildren and great-grandchildren) and friends becomes infinitely easier via the Internet.

Bring all other electronic lines of communication up to speed. Buy a home phone with large numbers and increased volume, and place it in the room that your elder occupies most frequently, preferably in the bedroom. Make sure there's a list of emergency phone contacts near each phone and posted on the refrigerator. Buy your elder a cell phone if necessary, if you want to have the ability to locate him or her immediately. Consider installing surveillanceware if your elder is usually alone or if you want to maximize your safety awareness. It has to be installed with your elder's consent. Other elder-friendly electronic enhancements include phones with increased volume and ring tones for the hearing impaired, as well as camera phones that allow you to see each other while speaking on the phone. These products break down communication barriers and make it easier for your elder to avoid emotional and physical isolation.

Most communication devices have adaptive extensions that can help anyone with any sensory loss or diminished sensory capacities. Whatever devices you are using, contact the customer care center of the manufacturer.

Be Honest with Yourself

Caring for an elder loved one is an incredibly stressful job. To have any chance at being a powerful caregiver, you have to be honest with yourself. What are you willing to sacrifice, if anything? Know your limitations, energy level, time constraints, family obligations, and work commitments. Your life has to go on. What are you not willing to do? In order to have something to give, you have to have something in the personal well. Answering these questions honestly will lead you to hiring and delegating properly so that your reserve doesn't run dry. You have to do everything in you power to meet your elder's needs.

Stay Calm

Stay calm and centered in order to deal with the inevitable crises that come along. Take care of yourself so that you can be more proactive and less reactive along the winding road. Find a daily mechanism that brings you to a centered, balanced place. I like to exercise or spend time in my garden. Others enjoy spiritual meditation. Creative pursuits such as painting or writing help, too. Any activity that gives you a sense of balance will increase your tolerance and energy level. Many elder care problems don't have an easy or immediate solution, and as long as you stay calm and centered, you'll be better able to manage these challenges.

Step 1: Communicate Openly

You should have someone outside of your family to talk to, someone who won't judge you and who isn't a part of your family history. If there's nobody available or you dislike therapy, I strongly suggest that you keep a journal of the experience. Keeping perspective will help you stay balanced and give you more energy for yourself and your elder.

Don't Be a Martyr

Most important, do not become a martyr! You'll only become resentful and unproductive, and your elder's care will suffer. I've even seen caregivers who become so overworked and overwhelmed that they get sick and pass away before the person they're caring for does.

I was involved with a young California family that was trying to take care of three elderly relatives who lived in different New York City locations. The Californians had tried to deal with all of the doctors, helpers, and aides, as well as the nursing home applications, and medical and insurance forms. They were flying back and forth, spending their own money, and becoming more and more frustrated with their elderly relatives who expressed some hostility, were reluctant to give information, and were resentful about the "giving up" of independence. The Californians felt like martyrs.

The elder New Yorkers didn't understand how much time, effort, and money was being spent on them by this young couple. Everyone felt justified in his or her accumulated resentment. When the Californians got in touch with me, I quickly organized their elders' information. I then opened up the lines of communication so that everyone understood what the others were doing, why they were doing it, and what the goals, objectives, fears, and anxieties were. We finally reached some common ground. The Californians began to see how their efforts, though well intentioned, were being perceived by their three elderly relatives. In turn, the elderly understood how much they truly needed the help, and they were more forthright and honest with their information.

All too often, I see caregivers play the martyr when what they should do is ask for help. As long as you determine exactly what help is needed, most people will be eager to come to your aide. Take care of yourself first, and then determine the time and resources you can devote to elder care. What you cannot handle should be taken on by your relatives and other important people in your elder's life. If your cousin works in construction, ask him to fix the creaky stairs; if you have a lawyer in the family, see if he or she can help with your elder's will and health care proxy; and so on. Even a referral to another professional in his or her field can save you time and aggravation. Others can offer a financial contribution or a specific talent (like balancing a checkbook or painting the home), or just stop by every other Saturday afternoon. Most requests will be met as long as you have a specific time frame and task in mind.

I know you feel scared, angry, guilty, and alone, but you're not. Be sure to rely on others for moments of relief. Caring for an elder loved one can be an overwhelming job, and you can't do it all by yourself. Get support from and delegate to others. Don't let yourself become caught in a no-win situation.

Communicating with Family Members and Others

It's crucial that all interested and involved relatives, friends, and others have the same understanding regarding your elder's care. Trust your instincts. If you feel something is wrong, check it out. Speak with your elder's neighbors, landlord, doctors, and friends. Broadening the lines of communication will give you a more complete picture of your elder's true condition and allow you to be an informed caregiver.

Don't Keep Secrets

Often, the biggest mistake a family makes is keeping secrets about their elder's care. I've witnessed the bitter disintegration of families over information that should be out in the open for all to understand. As the primary caregiver, you have the responsibility to manage the flow of information regarding your elder's condition and care. Every family situation presents a unique set of circumstances, but I'm telling you loud and clear that open communication is better than secrets.

Keeping family members in the dark in areas not vital for the safety and well-being of your elder should be avoided at all costs. Secrets lead to speculation, turmoil, and unnecessary conflict at a time that can already be especially trying for all involved. Everyone wants to be heard and understood. As soon as possible, bring family members into the loop regarding your elder's condition. Establish a chain of communication so that all who are interested and involved will have the most up-to-date information. Especially in the era of e-mail, it's relatively simple to send a mass message that keeps everyone informed.

LGBTQ Seniors

The Family Equality Council connects, supports, and represents parents who are lesbian, gay, bisexual, transgender, and queer (or often referred to as questioning) in this country and their children. They work to ensure equality for LGBTQ families by building community, changing hearts and minds, and advancing social justice for all families.

Many older LGBTQ adults came of age during a time when homosexuality and any gender nonconformity were criminalized, and many have remained invisible. Many of these older adults have spent the bulk of their lives concealing their sexual orientation and/or gender identity, with a major part of their life story ignored or invalidated. With this complex history, our older generations of LGBTQ individuals are different than the current generation and deserve special consideration. Terminologies have also changed and are continuing to change. Use the elder's words and terminologies that they use to describe themselves. Listen to their stories and be sensitive.

LGBTQ older adults are at risk for significant mental and physical health disparities. They have higher rates of anxiety, depression, and substance use disorders and also are at increased risk for certain medical conditions, such as obesity, breast cancer, and HIV.

Having worked in nursing homes, I have come across many stories where two same sex "roommates" of forty years were forced to deal with paperwork and family, thus the hidden secret of their lifestyle became evident and not always accepted even in their final days. Acceptance is such an important aspect of one's life, whether you are young or old.

Communicating with Professionals

As a caregiver, you often face a difficult challenge getting information from the professionals also dealing with your elder's situation. Whether it's a lawyer, doctor, social worker, or nurse, you might come to rely on his or her expertise to help your elder.

So how do you get accurate information from these professionals? You have to make them take you seriously. However, most professionals have little time, so you have to ask the appropriate questions. Do your homework and be prepared before you get them on the phone or meet in person. I usually skip the "Hellos" and "How are you's" and get right to the point. When possible, I write out questions ahead of time so I don't forget anything. This increases the likelihood that you'll get the real information you need. Ask questions like "Tell me exactly what is going on," "What are the side effects of that medication?" and "What is the time frame for recovery?" Professionals will be more likely to return your phone call if they know you're organized and won't waste their time. Please review the detailed list of the human anatomy, as well as the medical specialist associated with each body region. It could help your dialogue with health care professionals immensely.

Be sure to visit my website at www.doctormarion.com to access a wide array of elder care information, including a comprehensive list of the most up-to-date professional elder care resources available. It's my hope that you will use my website as a starting point for additional information and resources. Begin at the national level before seeking your state, city, local, and community resources for specific programs, aid, and guidance.

Step 2

Put Safety First

My mother fell in her home and had to spend time in the hospital. My family had no idea how to prepare for her discharge. We wanted to make her house safer, but we didn't want to restrict her mobility. Over time, we were able to adapt the house to meet my mom's needs. We also implemented the same improvements for our two other elderly relatives.
—R.J., in Florida

One of the first things I do after meeting a new client is visit the home and eliminate all potential hazards so that the environment is safer. Many elderly are victims of accidents in their own homes, and most of these accidents can be prevented with a few commonsense steps.

I've been to many of my clients' homes, and no matter how clean or organized they may be, there are almost always safety or hygiene issues that need to be addressed. I remember one client who was a brilliant writer and a charming and intelligent woman. But she lived in her own head; her place was a complete mess, full of clutter, dirt, peeling paint, and rodents that entered and exited via holes behind the refrigerator. The mice were so brazen that they danced on the table. My client even had names for them! My first reaction was to get her out of that environment and have the place fumigated and brought up to hygienic standards. She agreed to have the improvements done, but she wanted to stay in the home. Together we devised a weekly work schedule, and we stuck to the plan. It took almost three months, but the job was completed successfully.

In the process I was also able to install safety devices, such as tub and toilet railings, plus all of the other items that made it possible for her to live independently in her apartment much longer than she would have been able to otherwise.

Here are fifty-one ways to make your elder's home environment as safe as possible. Try to implement many, if not all, of these suggestions. There may be other necessary improvements that are unique to your elder. If you have any additional suggestions contact me on my website: www.doctormarion.com.

- Toss out throw rugs.
- Clean any remaining carpets.
- Replace door knobs and faucet handles with easy-to-grab levers (including different textures for each room and fixture).
- Replace glass shower doors with shower curtains (which should be changed every six months).
- Affix non-slip strips to the bathtub floor.
- Affix non-skid bath mats to the bathroom floor.
- If the stove has removable knobs, replace them with permanent knobs.
- Clearly label all water faucets "hot" and "cold."
- Put all appliances, dishes, and silverware where they're easy to reach.
- Use unbreakable dishes.
- Program telephones with emergency numbers: doctor, fire department, police, your phone, and so on.
- Plan and practice using an emergency escape route in case of fire.
- Subscribe to a personal safety response service in case of emergency.
- If anything in the home is broken (window, stove, floor tile, door lock), fix or discard it.
- Make sure all smoke detectors are in perfect working condition.
- Change locks on all doors and windows.

Step 2: Put Safety First

- Install radon and carbon monoxide detectors.
- Repair broken tiles.
- Remove all knives, razor blades, and scissors.
- Use only nonflammable fabrics.
- Remove all poisons from the home.
- Put eye-level decals on glass and screen doors.
- Ventilate rooms properly.
- Close all rodent holes, and hire an exterminator if needed.
- Check the refrigerator for leaks that could rot wood floors.
- Use a gas stove so that it's easy to determine if the stove is on (you can see the flame with a gas stove).
- Use allergen-free bedding to reduce mite infestation and other allergy-causing agents.
- Increase the wattage on all lamps for better lighting.
- Buy an all-in-one remote control for the TV and playback hardware; then program it and show your elder how to use it.
- Secure all banisters and stairs.
- Use only clean air filters since dirty filters release dust and dirt particles into the air.
- Make sure there are solid chairs in the home.
- Add cushions to chairs for increased comfort and safety.
- Set faucet and tub water temperature to prevent scalding.
- Make sure the home thermostat is not set too high or too low, especially in summer heat and winter cold.
- Don't place items on stairs to be carried up at a later time.
- Consider installing gates on all staircases.
- Remove all clutter: if something does not serve a purpose, get rid of it.

- Remove interior locks on all doors to prevent your elder from locking him or herself in.
- Never hire a helper who smokes, since exposure to secondhand smoke seriously endangers an elder's health.
- Remove electric blankets.
- Move the washer and drier to the main floor to limit trips up and down stairs.
- Install at least one entry to the home that does not have steps.
- Install multi-level counters in the bathroom and kitchen for easier wheelchair access.
- Add outdoor lighting that can be controlled by motion sensors.
- Add a safety rail near the toilet.
- Add safety rails in the shower and tub.
- Watch for loose sleeves on clothing, which can catch fire during cooking.
- Install light switches at both the top and the bottom of any stairs.
- Make sure that any banister goes the full length of the stairs.
- Repair any steps that sag or wobble.

Pet Care

A few words about pets. Many elderly have pets that they love, and often a pet is their only daily companion. It's often easier for your elder to express affection for a pet than for family members. Pets have been proven to reduce blood pressure and stress and to relieve depression. So, feel free to keep healthy pets around, and be sure to put their food and water in a safe place.

Some pets, though, can cause problems. For example, if dogs aren't regularly let outside, they'll urinate and defecate in the home. In addition, elderly have been known to trip and fall over pets. If pets are kept, make sure they're being fed and given regular exercise, and are otherwise taken care of. Hire a walker if necessary. If regular feeding and exercise for your elder's pet cannot be achieved, you should find it a new home. But think long and hard before getting rid of a favorite pet. Your elder may really need the contact.

Prepare for Emergencies

It's important to prepare for emergencies with backup generators, extra oxygen, sanitary supplies, medications, signed prescriptions from the doctor, food, water, flashlights, batteries, a battery-operated radio, a handheld can opener, a small camping blanket, and a plastic raincoat or poncho. Keep a backpack for each member of the household that is ready to go at a moment's notice.

Safety Tips for Outside of the Home

Many elderly are staying more active later in life, and that's great, but it has also resulted in a sharp increase in elder-related crimes. Following are many safety tips to consider when your elder ventures outside the home.

- Wear shoes that are comfortable and in good repair.
- Carry a purse or wallet with a firm grip and keep it close to your body.
- Put a rubber band around your wallet and put your wallet in an inside pocket if possible.
- When shopping, use a cart, because it can help with balance.
- Don't attempt to carry too many goods home; you can often have packages delivered.
- Don't leave notes on the exterior of the door when going out.
- Leave the light, the TV, or the radio on in the home.
- Have your keys in your hand when you arrive home or when you are approaching your car.
- If you must ask for directions, yell them out from a distance.
- Don't wear headphones; they are distracting and can cut you off from your environment.

- Take your medication with you if you will be gone for an extended period of time.
- Carry a whistle, and if you think you're being followed, blow it or yell "Police!" or "Fire!" to get attention.
- While driving, put any purse on the passenger-side floor, out of sight, or in the back if you can reach it easily.
- Keep the windows up when you are driving.
- Don't open the trunk of the car when others are around you.
- When possible, travel well-lit streets and highways, or travel during daylight hours.
- Let someone know where you're going and the route you plan to take.
- Keep emergency items in the car, such as a hat, sunblock, a shovel, bottled water, a battery charger, a spare tire, a flashlight, an umbrella, maps, blankets, and gloves.
- Try to keep a cell phone (with charger) with you in case of an emergency.
- When banking, be aware of who is around the automated teller machine, and use direct deposit when possible.
- Count your money during all transactions.
- Keep money out of sight and in a safe place.
- Never leave your valuables unattended.

Outdoor Safety

Your elder also needs to be safe when outside the home. Just crossing the street can be an adventure. I was in Manhattan with two clients of mine, a ninety-five-year-old man and his eighty-eight-year-old wife. Traffic was roaring past us on the street when suddenly the man stepped across two lanes of traffic. He was nearly hit. He looked back at us, smiling, and his wife yelled across, "You think you're eighty-five again!"

Now, I don't mean to detract from the seriousness of what could have happened. I just want you to realize that seniors don't lose their sense of humor. Tell your elder to be aware of the surroundings and to walk with confidence. Take every precaution when traveling with your elder. Please *see* Step 7: Find Mobility in Disability for a more frank discussion about this subject.

Step 3

Improve the Lifestyle

Our father was suffering with Alzheimer's, so we tried a bunch of fun family activities to improve the situation. He also attended an adult day care center that had an Alzheimer's group. It was amazing how much his spirits were lifted, and so were ours.

—G.H., in New York

For many elderly, Sunday turns into Monday which turns into Sunday, and the next thing they know, a week has gone by, then a month, then a year. Time flies, but it's not much fun, and you know why? Every day is the same, right down to the number of pills being taken. Most elderly have very little communication with the outside world. They don't exercise, they have nothing new to talk about, and for some, even the food they eat is the same day in and day out. Many elderly suffer from a lack of mental and physical stimulation, so naturally, the mind and body wither away. Increasing your elder's mental and physical stimulation is a focal part of your caregiving responsibility. You're in charge of rekindling life where the flame is flickering. I had a client who was clinically depressed. She had lost interest in friends, family, her local senior center, and her volunteer organization. She was seventy-three, and her family was concerned about the changes in her attitude and her disinterest in all of her former hobbies.

After an introduction and an in-house evaluation, she talked to me about her low interest level. She was cut off from things, frustrated, and angry. She found her own behavior baffling, but she said she could not seem to "get a jump start on life anymore." We started slowly by finding out about her former interests. She had enjoyed museums, so I brought in art magazines and art films. She was open to purchasing a DVD player and a larger TV, which also made closed captioning easier for her to read since she had severe hearing loss. She also consented to a phone that was equipped for the hearing impaired, which allowed her to better communicate with others. Reinvigorated, she agreed to physical exercise under the direction of her physician. This included breathing exercises with a yoga teacher. This approach worked wonders. Within a six-month period she was visiting her local senior center again. Sometimes we have to bring the world to our seniors before they will rejoin the world. It's usually well worth the time and effort.

Focus on Your Senior's Interests

Begin by discussing your elder's bucket list. If they are unable to travel or satisfy a bucket wish list, be creative. Find a way of bringing that experience to them. My brother-in-law, Bert, had always dreamed of going to Machu Picchu, but became too ill to travel. I went to the local library and borrowed movies and books about Peru, that we watched and read together, we went out for Peruvian food and I called the Peruvian embassy to send posters. When I went to Machu Picchu with a friend, I took along Bert's letters to me and burned them, sprinkling the ash into the wind.

Everyone has the same twenty-four hours. If your elder is on the decline, it's your job to encourage him or her to take advantage of time. Think of it in these terms: What if your elder had only one month to live—what would he or she want to do? Have your elder name three wishes and try to fulfill them if possible. Discover the obstacles and try to remove them.

This step is especially important if you, like most caregivers, are dealing with someone who's moving slowly into old age and still has some vitality remaining. Any type of activity you encourage will give your elder something to talk about, to anticipate, and to enjoy! This can improve spirit and overall disposition more than you can imagine. You must find ways to keep your elder engaged in the world and stay connected with family and community.

Americans are working later in life than ever before. According to data from the Census Bureau and Bureau of Labor Statistics, as of February 2019, about 20 percent of Americans over age sixty-five—a total of 10.6 million people—are either working or looking for work, representing a fifty-seven-year high.

The truth is that I don't have a specific formula. You should follow your intuition, and a clear path will present itself. Above all, try to strike the right balance. If your elder loves movies, bring him or her videos and DVDs, and enjoy a matinee together every so often. If your elder loves to eat, spice up life with a variety of new foods as well as favorite dishes from the past (always be sure to take the medical condition into account and what foods aren't allowed to be consumed; if in doubt, contact the doctor). If your loved one always wanted to paint but never had the chance to do it, now's the time to get to it. You'll be pleasantly surprised by how a little effort can result in a dramatically improved lifestyle.

Sample Skill Inventory

With every client, I gather a sample skill inventory. You have to know someone's background in order to help improve the quality of life. This is a basic checklist that reveals who someone is, what his or her hobbies are or were, and what other areas he or she may be interested in exploring or learning about. The answers you get will begin to point you in a clear direction so you can help improve your elder's quality of life. This list can trigger old interests and memories, and can lead to new hobbies as well. Going through this exercise often gives your elder increased energy and awareness. I always ask my client to check off any activities he or she has taken part in regularly, and to put a star next to any that he or she has organized or directed. Review this skill inventory list to find fun, engaging activities for your loved one. Connect with personal history and get in touch with their positive concepts, by asking them questions about their life: work, recreation, education, leisure time, and special interests. The idea is to connect with treasured moments and memories that they covet. Most people will share if it is done in a sharing and inclusive environment.

Skill Inventory List

Aquatics

- Boating
- Cruises
- Life guarding
- Swimming
- Water skiing

Art

- Cartooning
- Clay modeling
- Finger painting
- Oil painting
- Photography
- Scrapbooking
- Sculpture
- Sketching
- Watercolor painting

Character Building

- 4-H
- Big Brother/Big Sister mentoring
- Boy Scouts
- Campfire Girls
- Coaching sports
- Girl Scouts
- Religious groups
- Teaching (for example, Sunday school)
- YMCA
- YWCA

Clubs

- Athletic
- Collecting
- Craft
- Dramatic
- Literary
- Music

Crafts

- Basketry
- Ceramics
- Knitting
- Leatherwork
- Metalwork
- Model building
- Paper work (crepe, cardboard)
- Origami
- Pottery
- Woodwork

Dancing

- Aerobics
- Ballroom
- Folk
- Pilates
- Social
- Square
- Tap
- Zumba

Drama

- Dramatics
- Live Theater

Skill Inventory List (Continued)
Drama (Continued)

- Pageantry
- Storytelling
- Watching movies
- Watching TV

Games

- Active games
- Board games
- Card games
- Casino games
- Circle games
- Grand marches
- Online gaming
- Party games
- Progressive games
- Relay games
- Singing games
- Tag games

Gym Activities

- Calisthenics
- Gymnastics
- Pyramids
- Rope skipping
- Tumbling

Miscellaneous

- Adult Education
- Civic action
- Cooking and baking
- Driving
- Journalism
- Museums and galleries
- Public speaking
- Spas
- Teaching what you know at schools and youth groups
- Toastmasters International
- Volunteering
- Yoga

Music

- Band
- Barbershop singing
- Community singing
- Concerts
- Musical instruments
- Orchestra part singing
- Piano

Office

- Bookkeeping
- Computers
- Dictaphone work
- Filing
- Mimeographing
- Shorthand
- Typing

Outdoors

- Biking or cycling
- Bird watching
- Camping
- Fishing
- Gardening
- Hiking
- Nature study
- Snowmobiling

Skill Inventory List (Continued)
Sports

- Archery
- Badminton
- Baseball
- Basketball
- Bocce ball
- Bowling
- Boxing
- Coaching
- Curling
- Football
- Golf

- Hockey
- Horseshoes
- Skiing
- Soccer
- Softball
- Swimming
- Tennis
- Track
- Volleyball
- Wrestling

I always ask my client to list any additional hobbies or activities that aren't included in the skill list. I can't tell you how many times going through this list has helped my client recapture a sense of self. It helps him or her be happy about past strengths, and not be overwhelmed by a current weakness or sickness.

I was once contacted by a family who said their mother was noncommunicative after two years of being in a deep depression. The first thing I did was go through this sample skill inventory. I quickly learned that she had been a librarian and still adored books. So, I went to her local library and found a program where senior citizens were brought in to read to children each month. After some prodding, I took my client to the library, and she quickly became the program's most enthusiastic participant. Her family told me reading to the children was the highlight of her final years. She finally had something new to talk about. I would never have found something appropriate for my client to enjoy if I had not tried to discover her interests.

Nutrition

It is estimated that one in four seniors suffers from some level of malnutrition. Poor nutrition exacerbates existing illnesses and increases the risk of other illnesses such as pneumonia, osteoporosis, obesity, high blood pressure, diabetes, heart disease, certain cancers, and gastrointestinal problems. Poor nutrition also contributes to mental confusion. Those who are at risk for malnutrition are those:

- Over the age of seventy
- Who live alone and are housebound
- Who have a poor appetite and don't eat balanced meals
- Who live on a limited budget

Other factors can also contribute to inadequate nutrition. Poor health may result in one's not eating well; similarly, medications for ailments may diminish appetite. It's estimated that nearly one-third of seniors produce less stomach acid, resulting in nutrients not being thoroughly absorbed by the body. Other physical issues, such as difficulty with chewing or swallowing can affect eating habits, too. Finally, feeling lonely or depressed can suppress an elder person's appetite.

Many elders don't get anything resembling a balanced meal. Find out if Meals on Wheels or any meal program in your community is available in your town, and ask if your elder would like to receive such meals. If your elder has a favorite local restaurant, investigate whether the restaurant delivers to residences. Some grocery stores offer a hot meal service as well. You can set up a account ahead of time. What's better than a knock at the door and a hot lunch and dinner delivered each day?

Food may be one of the few remaining varieties in your elder's life. It might be more important now than ever before, so it's crucial to fill the house with food that your elder likes, as long as it's approved by the doctor. Consider likes and dislikes and shape a diet accordingly. Now, I'm not a nutritionist, so first I check with my client's doctor to see if there are any dietary hazards. I then make sure proper nutritional needs are met based on age, height, and weight. Many elderly will lose interest in food and just not eat enough. This won't happen if you keep food fresh and interesting. Even consider hiring a geriatric nutritionist to design appropriate meals.

Make sure your elder's diet is customized, based on his or her needs. Carefully check the labels on all food products. Does your elder require sodium-free food? Be sure to ask all of the right questions as dietary needs and problems change as a

Eating Well as We Age

Issue: Can't Chew

Instead of	Try
Fresh fruit	Fruit juices, soft canned fruits such as apple sauce or pears
Raw vegetables	Vegetable juices, creamed and mashed cooked vegetables
Meat	Ground meat, eggs, milk, cheese, yogurt, soups, pudding
Sliced bread	Cooked cereals, rice, bread pudding, soft cookies

Issue: Upset Stomach

Instead of	Try
Milk	Dairy products such as soups, pudding, yogurt, cheese
Vegetables	Vegetable juices, green beans, carrots, potatoes, cabbage, broccoli
Fresh fruit	Fruit juices and soft canned vegetables

Issue: Can't Shop

Ask local stores to deliver.

Ask church/synagogue members or volunteer services to deliver.

Ask a friend or family member to shop.

Pay someone to shop.

Issue: Can't Cook

Use a microwave oven for frozen dinners.

Take part in group meals offered by senior centers.

Have meals, such as Meals on Wheels, or any such program, brought to you.

Move to a senior home or relative's home where someone else cooks.

Issue: No Appetite

Dine with family or friends.

Take part in group meal programs.

Ask your doctor if medications are affecting appetite.

Issue: Short of Money

Buy low-cost foods.

Use coupons when shopping.

Buy foods on sale.

Check on low-cost meals through religious groups or senior centers.

Take part in meal programs for seniors.

Use food stamps.

Source: Food and Drug Administration

person ages. At all times, keep the doctor informed as to what the elder is or isn't eating.

When preparing foods, I rely on a few commonsense rules. First, I prepare foods from all of the different food groups. Second, I use an interesting color palette such as a plate with red, green, white, yellow, and brown foods. Try this and you'll see you've probably covered the major foods groups. Third, I firmly believe that fresh foods are crucial. If something has been out of the ground more than four days, much of its nutritional value has been lost. I rarely use canned or frozen foods. Keep food fresh, and your elder will greatly appreciate it. So will his or her body and mind.

Also remember that water is the "forgotten nutrient." Many seniors suffer from dehydration simply because they do not take in adequate fluids. The thirst urge often diminishes as we age, so dehydration can sneak up on us. Make sure your elder drinks plenty of water; if water is boring, add natural flavors, substitute juices, herbal teas, and other nutrition drinks.

When cooking at home, take turns being the boss and letting your elder come up with the recipe. Find your elder's favorite cookbook and turn to the most worn page—that's the favorite recipe. Prepare it.

Discourage packaged foods. Most of the nutrients have been stripped away. Your elder needs the vitamins and minerals now more than ever to stay healthy and active. Involve your loved one in the shopping process. Make a list and buy exactly what he or she wants. Take him or her with you to the store or outdoor farmer's market if it's not too cumbersome a task. Emphasize independence whenever possible. Use the electric cart that's often provided by the store for elderly or disabled persons.

Extra precautions should be taken when preparing food. Cook meat more thoroughly to decrease chances of bacterial infection. Your elder's immune system might have a lower resistance to infection. Check packages and labels for expiration dates. Sometimes these dates are hard to read, but they are worth checking. Inspect fresh food for mold and open packages or cans that are dented. When the meal is finished, dispose of the waste in a quick and proper fashion. Replace sponges and dish towels on a regular basis to limit the presence of bacteria, too. Change the tablecloth often and wipe down all surfaces.

Does your elder have impairments that make eating difficult? Feeding ourselves helps us maintain our dignity. Plan a diet and eating routine that allows for physical impairments as much as possible. If your elder has lost some manual dexterity, encourage finger foods and smaller portions. Use unbreakable plates. You have to make eating elder-friendly. I often prepare foods so that my client can eat with his or her fingers and there's absolutely nothing wrong with that. It allows your elder to maintain more independence. I often recommend softer foods and soups. This is another way to make food more easily digestible. It also helps elderly who have dentures, gum problems, or other dental issues.

In case of emergency, you should have enough bottled water and nonperishable food for your elder to remain comfortable overnight or longer if necessary. Remembering to open a window after a blackout to allow air circulation can save a person's life. Don't take this issue lightly. Weather, crime, blackouts, and natural disasters do occur and should be considered, especially if your elder is not very mobile.

Balance in Minerals and Vitamins

The human body requires specific levels of both vitamins and minerals in order to function correctly. You can maintain proper vitamin levels by eating a healthy, well-balanced diet in accordance with nutritional guidelines outlined by the Food and Drug Administration.

A general practitioner has the ability to request blood tests that can diagnose a wide variety of vitamin deficiencies. Some deficiencies, however, may be the result of a specific disease or blood disorder, such as Crohn's disease, celiac disease, kidney disorders, or alcoholism. In this case, the medical provider may refer you to a specialist.

A dietitian typically helps you plan a balanced diet and advises you about the use of vitamin supplements. If your deficiency is the result of a disease or medical disorder, you may be referred to a medical specialist as well as a dietitian.

Nutritionist

Dietitians and nutritionists are not typically physicians, but are experts in nutrition. They often have master's or doctoral degrees in nutrition and can advise you about proper diet, how food can affect your overall health and weight issues.

Bariatric Physician

Bariatric physicians study obesity, its causes, and its prevention. A bariatric physician is well-prepared to provide you with in-depth nutritional information and information about exercise.

Endocrinologist

Endocrinology is the study of glands and the hormones that secrete them. A variety of hormonal conditions can contribute to obesity. These include hypothyroidism, polycystic ovary syndrome, and Cushing's disease. If you suffer from an endocrine system–related disorder, your doctor may refer you to an endocrinologist before referring you to a weight loss specialist or advising nutritional modifications.

Medications

It is crucial that seniors or their caregivers take an active role in the proper use of all prescription medications. People sixty-five and older make up 17 percent of the U.S. population, yet they take 35 percent of all prescription drugs sold in the United States. Moreover, nearly half of all adverse events from medications occur with people over the age of sixty. What causes these adverse events? It could be taking too many medications, negative drug interactions, and increased sensitivity to medications. As we age, our cellular structures change, and we're more sensitive to medications. For example, an eighty-five-year-old person will be more sensitive to a medication than a sixty-five-year-old.

Be sure to keep medications in a safe place, being aware of the safety of children or a visitor who may be helping themselves to your medication.

Over-the-counter drugs must be considered, too. When you take into account drugs prescribed by a doctor, and what your elder may also be taking over-the-counter, the amount of medication can really add up. Being overmedicated can have a disastrous effect on mental and physical well-being. Immediately take a careful inventory of all medications. Note the following questions.

- What is prescribed?
- Who prescribed it?
- What is the amount prescribed?
- What is the dosage?
- What is it taken for?
- How often is it taken?
- When is it supposed to be taken?
- Who pours the medications?
- Who ensures the stock of medications is not depleted?
- What over-the-counter medications are being taken?
- Does the doctor know about all of the over-the-counter medications?
- What vitamins are being taken?
- Are any medications contraindicated?
- Does each doctor know about all of the medications being taken?

I'm not a physician, so I always take all of this information to my client's doctor and thoroughly discuss all prescriptions, vitamins, and over-the-counter items. You should do the same. Ask the doctor if any of the medications are not recommended for your elder, and also ask about side effects. If some medications are eliminated, ask if they should be stopped immediately or if your elder should be carefully tapered off the drug. Ask if the medication is addictive. Keep a written list of all medications being taken. Show this list to the doctor during doctor visits or during a hospitalization.

Use a Medication Box

Be sure your elder has a user-friendly medication box. The bigger the better so it's easy to remove the pills. Add large labels to medicine bottles and arrange them with your own system to keep dosage times in order. You can use whatever works for you; just be consistent. I've seen husbands take their wives' medication and vice versa. This is the sort of thing you should try to avoid. Keep the medications in a safe place. Try to buy prescription medicines and over-the-counter drugs from one main pharmacy; it will help with familiarity and convenience. A pharmacist who is familiar with your elder's history can also help avoid contraindicated prescriptions. (Pharmacists can look up to see if a prescription is contraindicated with any other medications your elder is already taking. If there is an issue or problem, all your elder's doctors must be notified. Also what is best way to eliminate the problem or find a safe alternative for the elder?)

If you're traveling, be sure to take an extra roster of medications and written prescriptions with you. Medications can easily be lost or ruined along the way. One client of mine had an entire box of medications fall in the toilet and he had to be rushed to the hospital to replace his pills. Be prepared for this type of mishap. Also bring extra glasses or the eye glass prescription in the event that they're lost or broken.

Often, when your elder starts a new medication, he or she might experience some side effects or new symptoms. It could be as simple as an upset stomach or as worrisome as blurred vision or uneven equilibrium. Monitor any new problems for ten days. Ask the doctor if it's just a side effect or another level of symptoms. Often, the side effect will dissipate within five to seven days. I can't tell you how many times I've seen one of my clients experience these sorts of side effects, only to be put on another medication to treat the side effects. It can be sheer lunacy unless you're on top of the situation.

Finally, be very careful with medications prescribed for pain, anxiety, or sleeping. The effects of these drugs tend to linger longer in seniors and can make them groggy and much more susceptible to falling.

If you're not familiar with various medications, there are several good books that can be used for research, including *The Physician's Desk Reference* at www.PDR.net. In addition, most medications come with an information sheet, and the pharmacy should be able to provide more details per your request.

Physical Exercise

The body was meant to move. Exercise relieves stress, augments your coping abilities, wards off exhaustion, allows your body to function more fully, and changes your metabolism to help keep weight consistent. It can also increase the power of the natural immune system for better overall health. Harmony and balance are also achieved through physical activity, so encourage your elder to exercise at every turn, but be sure to consult with your elder's doctor before starting any physical exercise program.

Concentrate on abilities, not disabilities, when determining the best approach. It can be as simple as a short walk, or as thorough as ninety minutes of yoga. Always include a warm-up period before any exercise, as well as a cool-down period afterward. Dancing, tai chi, walking, Pilates, Wii activities, bowling, tennis, light strength training, isometric exercises, and swimming are also all effective options. On social media, meet up groups are a great way to find group activities that are designated by interest, sometimes age, and abilities.

Be sure your elder drinks enough water on a daily basis and when exercising. This will ward off dehydration, and can be the simple cure for headaches, nausea, and even exhaustion. Avoid caffeinated drinks such as coffee, tea, and especially soft drinks. Consult your elder's physician to be sure about the adequate amount of liquids for his or her age, weight, and height.

If your elder is unable to partake in any physical activity, take him or her outside in a wheelchair as often as possible. Fifteen minutes of sunlight per day will keep the inner clock ticking and energy and spirits up. Avoid sun downing—a phenomenon where days and nights become confused. Sunlight also provides natural vitamin D. Without it, humans become sad, paranoid, and even suicidal. Exposure to moderate amounts of sunlight improves a person's disposition dramatically. Even sitting by a window will make a difference. I use the rule when dealing with an aid of fifteen minutes of sun exposure on each side, periodically.

For a more detailed explanation of the available therapies, *see* Appendix B: Alternative Therapies. Again, remember that no therapies should be tried without the consent of your elder's attending physician. Understanding specific medical specialties is important in finding the right expert to support you in your changing needs.

Sports Medicine Doctors

Family physicians with special training in sports medicine try to improve patients' health and wellness and prevent illness and injury associated with exercise. In medical school, primary care sports medicine doctors study exercise physiology, nutrition, biomechanics, psychology, physical evaluation, and rehabilitative medicine. Sports medicine doctors treat sprains, strains, and chronic overuse problems such as tendinitis and fractures. If your injury involves the foot or ankle, your doctor may refer you to a sports medicine podiatrist.

Orthopedic Specialists

Orthopedic surgeons care for and operate on people who have problems with the bones, muscles, and joints.

Sleep

When you take care of sleep many other things will fall into line. Sleep helps us focus and gives us clarity especially in stressful circumstances. Sleep gives us the emotional, physical, and psychological strength to meet life's challenges. I believe we find hidden treasures in sleeping well: we can solve problems, we become more rejuvenated, and we can heal emotionally and physically. Sleep also gives us clarity. When you do not get enough sleep or if sleep is disturbed, you wake up feeling fragmented. Lack of sleep manifests itself in many ways. What I mean by this is problem solving becomes more difficult, we do not have as much energy, our dispositions may plummet, our patience dissipates, we may find ourselves less tolerant, and we are more inclined to engage in disruptive behavior. Sleep is important for all of us, especially for the caregiver and the elderly loved one.

Getting Adequate Sleep

How does one get a good night's sleep? Try the following tips:

Step 3: Improve the Lifestyle

- Following a ritual is so important in getting a good night's sleep.
- Turn the TV and other electronic devices off an hour before sleep.
- Reading is great, but find something with less suspense, cliffhangers, and action (you do not want to activate the imagination).
- Something warm to drink such as warm milk, warm milk and honey, warm water, or chamomile tea can bring us nighttime comfort. Make sure it is non-caffeinated.
- Making the physical environment comfortable—such as drawing the curtains, taking down light and noise. Night lights, though, may be important for safety.
- Taking a warm bath or shower for many is relaxing. Using pleasant bath salts and skin oils that bring pleasant memories or help us relax can be helpful in creating a restful night.
- Do not eat heavily before bed. This can keep us up at night.
- Having a favorite plush toy to hug or something that has pleasant memories can help us fall asleep with ease
- Using the right detergent for night clothing and bedding is important. Toxins from detergent and allergens such as down can affect a good night's sleep. I had a patient who had severe congestion at night that was severely affecting her sleep. When I looked at her bedding, she had down pillows from her grandmother. Old pillows have mold and bacteria, retain odor, and can have bugs. Make sure you look at your bedding, your family's bedding, and the bedding of your elderly loved one. Throw out old pillows, old comforters, and old mattresses!
- Noisy fabric can disturb sleep as well. Find natural and soft fabrics for bedding.
- Having something familiar on a trip can help you get a good night's sleep, bring your own pillow. Like a

kid with your own blanky, we all want to go into a comfort zone before we go to sleep no matter what age we are.

- We need to listen to our seniors when it comes to sleep. If they complain about sleep, it is important to hear them and also support them in finding the root of the problem.

I had a client who just could not sleep. He was irritated every night. When I asked him about his sleep ritual, he told me he spoke to his ex-wife every night before going to bed, whom he had divorced twenty years ago. Every night they would end in a fight. I suggested they speak at lunchtime instead. They did and his sleep became peaceful. Sometimes the obvious is the simplest solution and sometimes it is what we most often overlook.

Energize with a Visualization Exercise

I also use a visualization technique that allows my client to recapture some of the energy of youth. This works best when done for ten minutes every day. Play a relaxing type of music, or nature and/or wind sounds, and give your elder aural guidance, such as "You're now comfortable." I ask my client to close his or her eyes, and breathe deeply, in through the nose, then out through the mouth. After he or she is calm and centered, I go back to a happy time in his or her youth when my client felt especially good.

Once there, I request all of the details—the sights, the smells, the sounds, the people, and the situation, anything he or she can recall. Everyone can go back to at least one very positive moment from his or her youth, and most elders love to do so if given the chance. You'll be amazed at how much your loved one will brighten. After the visualization is over, your elder can often ride that positive energy for a long time. What does he or she get out of it? He or she sees the world from another perspective, which can be very enlightening at a time when he or she is eager to be enlightened. Your elder can also reclaim a sense of control, and feel that he or she is doing something good that gets to the core of who he or she is. Your loved one will look forward to the relaxation exercise because it provides these tangible mental benefits.

I had one seventy-eight-year-old client who had been depressed for weeks. During a visualization session, we came to a memory she had from her high school formal dance in 1946. While dancing with her dream date, she ripped her nylons. The young man encouraged her to take them off and dance barefoot, which she did with rebellious abandon. They caused quite a stir in the auditorium! She was thrilled by the memory, and talked about it for months afterward. Caregiving is often like guiding someone to a desert oasis, where memories are the water. Facilitate your elder's memory retrieval often, so he or she may drink from the fountain of his or her life. You'll be amazed by the stories.

I also often ask my clients to close their eyes, breathe deeply, in and then out, and begin a positive affirmation exercise. I say, "I'm at peace with my family." Then they repeat it. I say, "I'm content with my life." Then they repeat it. I say, "I have earned these wrinkles." Then they repeat it, and so on. There are guided imagery scripts available online for relaxation and stress reduction.

Creativity

Recent studies show that stimulating the brain through any creative process encourages other parts of the brain to retain its capacity. I know firsthand that creativity works wonders for the elderly. Whether it's singing, painting, playing an instrument, dancing, or writing poetry, a journal, or a novel, creativity keeps a person in the here and now. Getting in touch with the creative self allows your elder to stay connected to the wonders of life. Your loved one might even draw on creative impulses and abilities he or she never pursued or had the time to nurture.

One client of mine was a real street-smart tough guy. He started writing the most tender poetry at the age of eighty-nine. He entered a contest for poets over seventy-five, and he won! His poetry changed the way he looked at the world—and himself—and it did wonders for his outlook and energy level. Creative pursuits will give your elder something to look forward to and talk about. He or she could discover a new talent after all of these years. Your loved one will be in better spirits, enjoy improved mental acuity, gain a better appetite, and be more social.

Your elder could paint a self-portrait, sculpt a Greek goddess, or sing in a choir. Pick a project and see it through. Having a goal also helps people look forward to the next day. Group activities are especially enjoyable, too. This could include any number of activities, such as joining a choir or taking an arts and crafts class. The group can then become a crucial part of your elder's social network and support system. Consider these creative outlets:

- Painting
- Drawing
- Charcoal sketching
- Singing
- Writing music
- Playing an instrument
- Creative writing and short stories
- Writing poetry
- Writing in a journal
- Writing a novel
- Arts and crafts class
- Knitting
- Sculpture
- Oral storytelling
- Writing articles for a local paper or blog

Encourage any current creative hobbies or introduce new ones. They'll keep your elder's mind active. I love to sing, so often I'll find songs from a client's era and sing until one piques his or her interest.

One of my clients had been a housewife, a mother, and a seamstress at home to make money for her family. She never worked outside the home. After talking to her and seeing some of the designs she had sketched over the years, I was impressed with her creativity. Her family now wanted her to be involved with the local church or senior center, but she wanted to stay at home. I experimented with several ideas for activities or recreation, but she showed no interest until I encouraged her to sew again.

She could no longer sew, cut, or thread a needle, so I visited the local sewing, knitting, art supply, and yard good stores to buy all sorts of "end" items, odd buttons, heavy stock cardboard, and scraps of trimmings. I then encouraged her to make imaginative pictures, shapes, and color combinations. She took to it quickly, and was creative, structured, and diligent. She passed the hours away in her new creative efforts, as happy as she had been in her earlier years.

Entertainment

Your elder can become so focused on current hardships that he or she loses touch with the outside world. It is your job to bring the world to him or her in the form of books, movies, music, and other entertainment. I often see families who are baffled by what to do. C'mon, wake up! There's a limitless supply of things to do, especially in today's information age. Take the time to learn about your elder's likes and dislikes and go from there. Determine if he or she has a favorite author, actor, or singer, and bring some of the works of one of them. Reintroduce things he or she used to be interested in.

Even an afternoon stroll at the local mall to people-watch can be fun. Take him or her books movies from the library, or even download audio books. Catch an afternoon production if your elder is lucky enough to have a local theater nearby. Playing a board game for thirty minutes can also be a fun exercise. Find elderly discounts for early bird specials at restaurants and for movie and theater tickets. Hit the town as often as possible so he or she has something new to talk and think about and look forward to. When your elder is out of the house, he or she is more likely to forget about health problems and concentrate on the new images that are encountered. Have fun researching and drawing up a family tree. If writing is difficult, the information can be recorded on video. Tell family stories. It can be fun and enlightening to pass history down from generation to generation.

Consider entertainment culled from the following categories:

- Movies (at the theater or at home on Netflix, Amazon Prime, Kindle, iPad, Apple TV, DVD, or any other online source of programming)
- Books (including audiobooks)
- The library
- Newspapers
- Magazines
- Music
- Photography
- Gardening
- Live theater
- Restaurants
- Concerts
- Bowling
- Museums
- Playing cards
- Board games
- Art exhibits
- Sporting events

I had one client who had been extremely belligerent and noncommunicative with me for over two months, but I kept at it. Finally, knowing he was a veteran, I took him to a World War II photography exhibit. Voila! I had found our common ground. Within moments, he started talking all about his experiences there and his career as a photo journalist. We had a lot of fun together for the rest of the time he was with us. We did online courses and got DVD's from the teaching company for continued education, learning, and cognitive stimulation.

Social Interaction

Sit and talk with your elder as often as possible. Consider storytelling or guided fantasy. Facilitate interaction with the local community whenever possible. Often, seniors go to the doctor for a social life. Don't allow that to happen. Encourage your elder to send birthday cards to family and friends. I ask what the event or occasion is, and if he or she can't go out, I'll purchase the cards. If he or she isn't able to write, I'll have him or her dictate what I should write in the card and then I send it in the mail. Often, the recipient responds, which opens another avenue of contact and interaction for your elder.

With the computer, tablets, smartphones, as well as apps such as Skype and What's App, you can keep your elder involved with the family, keeping them up to date with current events and family gossip.

This can be as simple as spending time and doing more than just talking. On one winter day, a storm blew through town and left ten inches of snow behind. I took my eighty-eight-year-old client outside to throw snowballs. He felt like a kid again and couldn't stop giggling. We were outside for only five minutes, but he told the "snowballing" story for months afterward.

Take your child for a visit. If the child just got a report card, talk about it with your elder. Do anything to show your elder that he or she is still a vital part of the world. Isolation is one of the toughest realities of aging, and you should do all that you can to prevent it. Your loved one needs to feel that he or she is a part of the family and community at large.

Set a goal together that emphasizes communicating with the outside world. Many senior citizens today are telling their life stories and recording them on computers or video cameras for future generations. You'll learn an amazing amount about your elder and about life during this process. Involve your senior in a religious community or volunteer group.

One of my clients had been a published writer and poet, but now she was in a wheelchair and legally blind. She showed no interest in anything, not even her beloved opera music on the radio. She was too depressed about her inability to see and read. After much trial and error, I discovered that she liked being read to, so I hired a young high school student who wanted to be a writer and poet. This girl visited two times a week and lifted my client's spirits so much that eventually she was listening to Saturday afternoon opera again. Since her health was still relatively good, I would purchase wheelchair-accommodating seats for the afternoon performance at the opera. My client became much more communicative. One day she explained to me, "What I can't change, I must accept with grace."

Appearance

Often it has been years since anyone else paid attention to your senior's physical appearance. So, usually, your elder will appreciate any interest you show in it. Take him or her to the hairdresser or barber. Give him or her a regular pedicure and manicure. A facial is a real treat, too, if it's in the budget.

Look in the closet and toss out any clothes that are in tatters or disrepair, but always be sure to ask permission first. Make sure clothing is appropriate for the various seasons. If you find outdated styles or incorrect sizes, give them to a charity or throw them away. Make sure shoes are comfortable; at this stage of the game, one need not be a slave to fashion and should not wear heels that could cause a spill.

Take your elder shopping for new clothes and shoes. Look for Velcro closures, which are easier to fasten. Buy new makeup. I'm often shocked to find that many elderly women have either run out of makeup or have only lipstick that's several years old. If you have a teenage daughter, take her along and make a fun trip out of it for all three generations.

Encourage your elder to dress him or herself when possible. I had one client, an eighty-four-year-old gem of a man, who insisted that we install grab bars near his closet so he could still dress himself. He would say, "I'm still a man, Marion." I agreed with him wholeheartedly and made sure those grab bars were extra sturdy.

Buy your elder a hand mirror. It really does have a positive effect if he or she is conscious of appearance. Buy a new winter scarf. Polish shoes. Buy a new toothbrush. The little things make a big difference. Clean the wheelchair, walker, and/ or cane. Things you might take for granted have often been overlooked for years, and your elder will greatly appreciate the effort you make to improve appearances.

Intimacy

This may be surprising to some, but the vast majority of my clients are still sexually active. If they're not active, they're usually interested in the topic and enjoy talking about it. The need for affection, love, and physical recognition does not disappear as you get older. Don't be embarrassed if your parents are still active and interested in sex. Intimacy is powerful and it lives on as we age. In many ways, sex shows us who we are and reveals our deepest character.

Sex affirms our humanity, so be comfortable with it. Talk frankly about it with your elder if possible. It is beautiful when two people have aged well together and have kept a strong physical bond and sexual chemistry. Sex at an advanced age is all about touching, sharing, and feeling. Give your elder the space to experience it. Facilitate it and make sure your elder has privacy. This may not be easy to arrange, especially if your elder is in an institutional setting. Try to accommodate it anyway. If your loved one has a new partner, don't judge. Lastly, don't gossip about his or her sex life. Sex is a natural part of life, and your elder is entitled to privacy.

Spirituality

Many seniors believe there are forces at work in the universe, and many of them have tapped into some form of spirituality. They cannot understand everything that happens, and spirituality helps explain it. Even if spirituality is not discussed, it does exist in most people's conscious life. The connectedness to a spiritual life helps people deal with hardships and face fears, and, ultimately, can give them hope. A social community and support group can grow from organized religion. I find that most of my clients get a great deal out of their religious activities. It helps them feel that their life has a meaning and a purpose.

Every one of my clients, at one time or another, experiences an inner awareness or a quiet peace before they pass on. Even if fishing is their "religion" and something they love, they know where they need to go to find that quiet space for reflection, to recharge and gain perspective. This process helps our elders find a way to let go of emotions and worldly trappings, and become ready to travel free. A smile of a baby is joy, a sunset is quieting, a flower is refreshing, and a call from a friend is heartwarming. These experiences are most important.

Other Suggestions

Your elder should be acutely aware of the passing of time. Install a large, easy-to-read orientation clock that includes both the date and the time. Many seniors cannot read a digital clock, so they need an old fashioned round clock with twelve real numbers that are more readable and keep them more oriented to time. Also, have a calendar where he or she can mark off the days. This facilitates staying in the here and now.

I recommend labeling things all over the home because your elder might become frustrated by not remembering where clothes, silverware, or food belongs. Clear labels affixed to cabinets, drawers, and pantries could help immeasurably.

Find local businesses that cater to the elderly. You should be able to find services such as cooking, laundry, beauty needs, pet walking, and so forth. Do yourself and your elder a favor and hire these businesses when affordable and appropriate. They can greatly improve everyone's quality of life.

The body needs to be touched, and our skin is our largest organ. If it's affordable, hire your elder a massage therapist. If that's not feasible, take the time to rub your elder's hands, neck, shoulders, and feet, all of the places that you can reach easily. Always ask your elder if that's what he or she wants done, since not everyone is comfortable being touched.

Step 4

Make Life Easier with Adapted Equipment

We had no idea how to help our aunt and uncle deal with their declining health and thought processes. A friend led us to Doctor Marion, and under her guidance we purchased specially devised adapted equipment that helped my aunt and uncle maintain their independence. They were also able to regain some of their former abilities, like taking a shower, which greatly improved their quality of life.

—I.L., in Washington

Most people have no idea what *adapted equipment* is, but, as a caregiver, you should become aware of this growing field. I'm talking about commonplace products like a wheelchair or an elder-safe stepladder as well as more obscure products such as jar/bottle openers and grocery store scooters. Adapted equipment draws from a wide variety of products that can help your elder function more independently and/or on a higher level. Such equipment can help your elder regain confidence in his or her abilities, and can even alleviate your elder's overwhelming fear of being dependent on others. Along with advancements in medical technology and pharmaceuticals, adapted equipment has come a long way in recent years and can be a vital part of a senior's final years. Bottom line: Adapted equipment can greatly improve your elder's quality of life.

Caregiving is largely about helping your elder maintain as much control of life as possible, and adapted equipment can help accomplish this important goal. Consider any and all products that might improve quality of life, which will help your elder help him or herself. You have no idea how big a difference this can make.

I had a client who was confined to a wheelchair. According to his family, he had always been very active and a real outdoorsman; he loved camping, fishing, gardening, and barbecuing. But he felt cut off from his beloved natural environment and was embarrassed to have anyone see him "stuck" in his wheelchair. He also had limited use of his left arm. So, with the help of his friends, we built him a raised indoor garden with grow-plant lights and adapted gardening equipment. He was able to grow violets indoors, and this became his new passion. His friends also purchased adapted cooking equipment for him and he was able to again prepare simple meals. This encouraged him to invite people over once again for social events at his home. For his eightieth birthday, his family and friends purchased a wheelchair swing so he could enjoy the breeze on his face in his own backyard.

I'm thrilled by the recent advances in adapted equipment. Below are some of the most useful and technologically advanced adapted equipment products. You should also explore other catalogues and websites (many of which can be found in the Resources section of this book) because there are too many useful products available to mention. If you have any other resources you would like to share, please visit me at my website: www.doctormarion.com, so I may continue to update my list.

- Hospital beds and/or new mattresses to replace the old beds
- Silverware that is easier to hold
- China that prevents spills
- Glassware such as sippy cups that eliminate spills and sippy cups with double handles
- Cushioned wheelchairs (one for indoors that is more rigid to facilitate eating, and a second for outdoor activity)
- Walkers that fold in half or that have an attached seat

Step 4: Make Life Easier with Adapted Equipment

- A Hoya lift for the home to help move someone short distances, such as from bed to wheelchair
- Electric stairs for the home
- Cushions that can help prop up someone who cannot support him or herself
- Prosthesis
- Cane of the correct height and style
- Suction brushes for the bathroom to clean nails, and for the sink to clean vegetables
- Jumbo-digit handheld timers
- Talking food scales
- Food preparation boards
- Paring boards
- Jar and bottle openers
- Pizza rolling knives
- Flip spatulas
- Graters with suction feet
- Gardening tools
- Racks that hold playing cards
- Bowls with suction bottoms
- Pots with handles on both sides
- Easy-tip teapot pouring system
- One-handed can opener
- Trays with wheels that fold under for compact storage, also adjustable for reading/writing
- Scissors with one-handed grip
- Door gripper to hold open the door
- Handles for hard-to-reach places
- Door knob turners that press down in order to turn
- Writing aids with a special grip
- Multi-purpose suction-mouth sticks to turn pages, paint, or otherwise communicate

- Traveling pouches, bags, baskets, or caddies, as well as a pouch for a walker or wheelchair
- Bed rails
- Transfer boards to go from one place to another, such as from wheelchair to bed
- Lazy Susan with a swivel cushion to transfer in and out of the car
- One-stop step stool for transport
- Leg lifts and cast handles
- Bed pull-ups
- Battery-operated hoists that are attached to the ceiling
- Ramp lifts, floor lifts, car and home lifts, and portable ramps
- Cushions and suspension pads that take the pressure off of feet, elbows, and other parts of the body
- Motorized wheelchair van
- Grocery store scooters
- 600–1,000-pound capacity hospital beds and wheelchairs
- Portable commode to place near the bed at night
- Adult diapers and disposable briefs for incontinence
- Bed liners
- Flood-proof cushions for chairs
- Motion detectors
- Remote door alarm that sounds if someone tries to get in or out at night
- Stove-top fire extinguishers
- Bathroom flood alarms
- Easy medication dispensers
- Phone that allows incoming but not outgoing calls
- Waterproof seat protectors
- Bibs that go all the way to the lap
- Smoke detectors with a dual transmitter

- Panorama-view car mirrors to increase peripheral vision and cut glare
- TTY phones that type messages rather than using audio playback
- Telephone amplifiers
- Super-phone ringers
- Device that emits a mild beep on the phone
- Magnifiers for computer monitors
- Braille TTY system
- Alarm clock with a vibrator to put under the pillow
- Big-button calculators
- Cushions for side rails on beds
- Velcro that can be used in place of shoelaces, buttons, snaps, or zippers
- Long handle grabbers
- Back scratchers

Using Adapted Equipment

There is a proper way to use a walker, to sit in a wheelchair, and to get in and out of bed. Make sure you and your elder learn the proper form and functions. Even if someone has all of the best adapted equipment, it's your job to ensure that he or she knows how to use it to receive the full benefit from the apparatus. The pharmacy or surgical supply store can often demonstrate the proper use of most purchased equipment. The therapist who recommended the equipment is often available to show you and your elder the proper use and handling of the equipment as well.

I once had a family call to say they were desperate; their elderly uncle had them at their wits' end. He was unable to walk, and was mostly confined to a wheelchair. The family thought they had tried everything, and he had become extremely uncooperative. I quickly found out that he had three passions as a young man: square dancing, baseball, and bowling. He believed that he was no longer able to participate in them because of his lack of mobility, and he was not interested in any new avenues. I showed him that he could still be a part

51

of society in a wheelchair. I made sure his wheelchair was comfortable and clean, and we bought a few pieces of adapted equipment, including a motorized scooter, so he felt better about his situation.

With encouragement and perseverance, we were able to purchase baseball tickets with wheelchair seating, and he saw his first "real" game in over ten years, with two of his pals sitting right next to him. This experience opened him up to some more adventures. I also found a handicapped-accessible bowling alley. He bowled a little, and thoroughly enjoyed watching the other games. He was then ready to watch old movies, especially musicals and productions with elaborate dance numbers. These rekindled interests brought about some new friendships and led to a new interest in chess, which he had never played or even understood before. These activities gave him a renewed interest in life, and being with people lifted his and his family's spirits.

Follow your elder's treatment schedule, and understand that there are real psychological effects caused by disease and/ or disability. This is especially true for those suffering from another ailment related to the aging process. But as long as a person summons the strength to persevere, you might be surprised at his or her ability to adapt to or overcome physical and psychological challenges.

Visit the doctor and have any suitable adapted equipment prescribed to meet your loved one's needs. You may want to do some research before your visit since some doctors are unaware of the wide variety of useful adapted equipment that's available. You can buy these products at a surgical supply store or a pharmacy with a surgical supply ordering department. You can also order them online or by mail from a catalogue. It's important to have certain pieces of adapted equipment measured in order to fit your elder, such as a cane. That should be done by a trained occupational or physical therapist in your area. Finally, ask car manufacturers if they have other adapted equipment for individuals with special needs.

Step 5

Manage Financial Issues

My mother had been a bookkeeper who balanced her checkbook to the penny. But as she aged, her bill paying became erratic. Since we lived far away, we were totally unaware of the problem initially, but it became a crisis situation. We hired a financial expert, who sorted through the back taxes and bills to bring order to my parents' finances, and peace of mind to my entire family.

—S.B., in Tennessee

Your elder's financial situation can be a difficult issue to address. The very nature of the discussion calls his or her independence into question. More often than not, your elder will not have involved you in his or her finances. But those days are over the moment you become a caregiver. Address finances as soon as possible. The longer you wait, the more likely it is that problems will arise.

Usually, I'm called by a family who needs help. But in one particular case, an elderly woman called me directly to "help sort out her life." She said she had just been widowed and had no idea how to write checks or balance her check book. She didn't even know how much money she had or where it was. April 15 was around the corner, and she knew she needed to pay taxes, but she didn't know how to go about it.

I quickly got her in touch with a few professional financial advisors. At my insistence, she interviewed three. We gathered the information to take to the financial advisor, and then got an extension for her to pay the taxes. We found her husband's insurance information and were also able to deal with the Social Security paperwork. We made charts and lists so that she could confidently deal directly with her newly hired team, including a financial advisor, a tax accountant, and a lawyer. It was wonderful to watch her go from being dependent and confused to becoming independent with some organizational assistance and professional guidance.

Average life expectancy in America in 1900 was forty-seven years of age. By 2000 it had reached a record seventy-seven, and it continues to rise. Many elderly are outliving their savings because they did not plan to survive as long as they have.

I've attempted to simplify the way to go about this step as much as possible, because this can be an especially daunting task. I recommend that you do the following:

- Figure out your elder's assets.
- Determine monthly income.
- Add up all monthly expenses.

You should then know if your elder has enough money to live comfortably for the rest of his or her life. You'll also need to know which government programs your elder should apply for and the possible benefits.

But let me emphasize that due to the complexity of some financial issues, I highly recommend you rely on the advice and expertise of a skilled professional to guide you. Hire an accountant, an elder care lawyer, a financial advisor, or a tax expert. How do you find these professionals? You may locate them via the Better Business Bureau, word of mouth, or, better yet, someone who is connected to your family. It is well worth the fees you'll pay to understand exactly how to allocate assets. Tackling this step alone could lead to legal snarls and become a drain on your energy and your checkbook. Professional expertise will save you many headaches and could ultimately lead to significant savings of your elder's finances.

Determine Assets

Many of today's retirees are living ten years longer and more than they thought they would. This has created a difficult issue: They're outliving their resources. Protect your elder. Gather the facts for a clear picture of his or her financial situation. I often find myself playing the role of detective, since much of this information is difficult to come by. So, put on your detective's hat and let's get started.

First, add up possible assets from the following sources. There may be others, so take them into account as well:

- Checking accounts
- Savings accounts
- Stocks
- Bonds
- Rental property income
- Home owner property
- Safe deposit boxes
- IRAs
- 401(k)s
- Pensions
- Vehicles
- Hidden valuables

Hidden valuables, you might ask? This happens often. Some seniors hide cash and valuables and forget where they put them. You might be surprised how clever seniors can be when hiding cash and earthly treasures. They could be buried in the backyard, safety-pinned inside a winter coat, wrapped in tinfoil behind the radiator, or placed in a shoe box under the attic floor boards. Some elderly cut out the heart of a book and put cash and valuables inside, and then place the book back on the shelf.

Other popular hiding spots include behind picture frames and art work, in deep recesses of closets, in the back of a clothing drawer, under the cover of an ironing board, at the bottom of the hamper, inside socks, in a freezer, and inside the unexposed belly of a piece of furniture. It's your task to find these valuables. It's much better to discover them now and include them as assets in order to make your elder's life more comfortable today.

You need to get an exact accounting of assets. Ask if your elder has any promissory notes to pay off. If so, pay them off as soon as possible. On the flip side, find out if any assets have been borrowed but never paid back. If so, try to collect on them, and ask about any silent partnerships. Determine if there are any liens against any of your elder's property and take care of that if possible. Make sure you're always within the legal boundaries. Speak with an elder care lawyer and/or financial advisor for guidance and direction.

I had one client who supposedly had most of his financial and legal issues neatly organized, including bank accounts, marriage certificates, death certificates, and tax records. He was aware of his current financial situation, but he did not understand how to determine his living expenses due to physical problems and memory failure. Up to that time in his life, he had always handled his own finances. He kept all of his information in a box, but he knew he was changing and he wanted to be prepared for what he called "the unknown."

He wanted to go to a veteran's hospital for medical treatment, but he did not know or understand his rights as a World War II veteran. His honorable discharge papers were nowhere to be found, so we started to navigate the government programs to get duplicates made. We also discovered what services he was entitled to. Eventually, we filled out all of the required papers and he received the benefits. We then made a list of his property, the location of the deeds, and all other assets, which were organized on paper. We gathered information for his personal insurance, as well as his house and property. Eventually, he had his accounts, contact names, telephone numbers, and other pertinent information in an easy-to-access file. He gained confidence in his ability to handle his future.

Determine Monthly Income

Now determine your elder's monthly income. Carefully add up the following sources of income, as well as any others there may be:

- Pension
- Interest
- Dividends
- Annuities
- Other businesses
- Disability

- Current job
- Bonds
- CDs
- Rental properties
- Social Security
- Unemployment

Monthly Expenses

Now add up your elder's monthly expenses from these common categories (again, there may be others):

Step 5: Manage Financial Issues

- Mortgage and/or rent
- Equity loans
- Home maintenance
- Utilities
- Water
- Car payments
- DMV fees
- Clothing
- Medicine
- Monthly memberships
- Annual credit card fees
- Cleaners/laundry
- Car insurance
- Recreational vehicle insurance
- Insurance for valuable collectibles such as coins and stamps
- Home renter's insurance
- Business insurance
- Medicare insurance
- VA insurance
- Entertainment
- Books
- Hair dresser or barber
- Jewelry
- Liquor
- Manicures/pedicures
- Massage
- Other Lessons

- Property taxes
- Parking
- Condominium fees
- Phone
- Food
- Car maintenance
- Gas
- Shoes
- Legal fees
- Credit card debt
- Child support/alimony
- Pet food and care
- Boat insurance
- Disability insurance
- Homeowners insurance
- Property insurance
- Life insurance
- Medicaid insurance
- Long-term care insurance
- Vacation and travel
- Subscriptions
- Makeup
- Cable TV/Internet
- Pocket cash
- Facials
- Therapy Sessions

A Word about Insurance

Insurance matters can be confusing. Start by understanding exactly what your elder's various policies cover. Get the original documents if possible. Figure out who the agent is or was. You might find there are multiple policies, duplicate policies, or policies that are no longer needed. This is especially common with personal property that has depreciated over time.

Determine exactly what is covered and the level of coverage. You may find an insurance policy that allows you to hire an aide, a registered nurse, a geriatric care manager, or a licensed social worker. Is respite care included? Or hospice? Ask questions and comparison shop where appropriate. Eliminate all excess and/or overlapping insurance, and be sure to fill out all proper forms in a timely manner. This can be a time-consuming process, but it'll save you money, time, and headaches in the future. Know exactly how insurance monies are dispersed when care is needed. Examine the difference between all different options of health care insurance and choose accordingly.

Finally, most elderly are satisfied with how they have lived their lives. However, I've observed that if they discover that they could run out of money, they feel like a huge failure. It's a real blow and often leads to depression. They have fought through war, disease, and all of the difficulties of life, but they get heartsick and internally conflicted at the thought that this could happen. Make sure you apply for Social Security, food stamps, veterans' benefits, Supplemental Security Income, and both Medicare and Medicaid if it applies. You will have a lot of paperwork to fill out, but the resulting funds are well worth the time and effort. They could make all the difference for everyone involved, especially your loved one.

Once on the case, make sure all bills are paid on time. Check to see if your elder is using automatic bill pay. Discontinue it if you're going to manually handle the finances from this point forward. Again, this process can be very time-consuming. If your elder is getting Social Security, is it being direct-deposited?

Again, I suggest hiring an elder care lawyer, accountant, or tax consultant to guide you through this long and often complicated process. It is well worth the cost to understand exactly how to manage all of the assets and papers in an appropriate and timely manner. Professional guidance may preserve your sanity in addition to saving your elder's estate thousands of dollars.

Reverse Mortgages

Reverse mortgage is an interesting option that was introduced just a few years ago. This is a legal document and should be looked at carefully. Here's how it works. Your elder sells his or her house to the bank after a fair appraised value has been agreed upon. The bank will then pay an agreed-upon amount each month until the house value has been exhausted. You should calculate the monthly payment so that it's as near to the monthly living expenses as possible, and not more, in order to make the nest egg last. If your elder passes away before the full value of the house has been returned, the heirs get the remaining cash, and the home remains the bank's property. Senior citizens over the age of sixty are eligible to apply for a reverse mortgage.

Long-Term Care Health Insurance

When it comes to long-term care insurance, refer to your own state's department of insurance. The phrase "long-term care" refers to the help that people with chronic illnesses, disabilities, or other conditions need on a daily basis over an extended period of time. The type of help needed can range from assistance with simple activities (such as bathing, dressing, and eating) to skilled care that's provided by nurses, therapists, or other professionals.

Employer-based health coverage will not pay for daily, extended care services. Medicare will cover a short stay in a nursing home, or a limited amount of at-home care, but only under certain conditions. To help cover potential long-term care expenses, some people choose to buy long-term care insurance.

Policies offer many different coverage options. Since you can't predict what your future long-term care needs will be, you may want to buy a policy with flexible options. Depending on the policy options you select, long-term care insurance can help you pay for the care you need, whether you are living at home or in an assisted living facility or nursing home. The insurance might also pay expenses for adult day care, care coordination, and other services. Some policies will even help pay costs associated with modifying your home so you can keep living in it safely.

When making choices about long-term care insurance it is important to do due diligence about the history and reviews of the insurance companies. A lawyer or financial advisor can be beneficial when reviewing these, or any, legal documents.

Other Issues

Figure out the cash value of the life insurance. Know the exact death benefit payout. Your elder can often receive a portion of the payout before death. After assessing all of this, you may want to add more life insurance. Ask a professional agent to provide detailed numbers for you.

Your elder should also have a clear tax plan in place. States have various timeframes, usually six months to one year, for when the tax bill must be settled. All new tax issues must be understood. Hire a professional to help you understand which assets go through probate and which do not (probate is when the state delays dispersing assets upon death and assesses a hefty tax). The state often collects without your having any say in the matter. Learn about it from a professional.

Provide for radical change such as an accident or advanced disease. If you can avoid doing so, never cut the monthly budget so close that an unforeseen accident would ruin your elder's finances.

If you need to contribute your own money to the cause, keep detailed records and receipts for every expense. Keep everything in chronological order, and write out a short justification for the expense. These bills can add up quickly, and the better the records you keep, the better the chance you have of being paid back.

Lastly, make sure all gift-giving decisions are well thought out. If gift giving is within your elder's means, all transactions should be reviewed and then executed under the advisement of an elder care lawyer or financial advisor. Above all, be sure your elder retains the means to live comfortably.

Step 6

Take Care of Legal Matters

*Soon after we realized our parents' mental capacities
were diminishing, we discovered that their legal papers were
out of date and other important documents were missing.
We hired an elder care lawyer who lived near them, and he
quickly got their legal papers in order. We then had our own
documents and advanced directives put in order to ensure
that our young child would be protected.*

—A.A., in Ohio

Just as you should be sure that all financial decisions are reviewed by an expert, all legal issues should be handled with the help of a trusted lawyer, accountant, or financial advisor, especially if there are complicated issues outside your scope of expertise. These issues include retirement timelines, tax advantages and disadvantages, tax planning, inheritance laws, asset protection, and federal and state financial rules and regulations. Many of the rules governing these issues fluctuate on a yearly basis and vary from state to state.

Discussing legal issues with your elder can be difficult, but you must forge ahead. Nobody likes a legal surprise, and it's time to get everything out in the open. Be proactive and find the right expert to serve your elder's need. The person you hire should not just be your elder's golfing buddy. You need a professional who has the skills and knowledge required to deal with the complexity of the situation.

I was called by an elderly couple who wanted to organize their household so that their children and grandchildren

61

wouldn't quarrel over their possessions after they had passed on. They were clear in their intent but did not know how to accomplish their goal. When I visited, I was overwhelmed by the assortment and volume of items. There wasn't a clear space to be found on the walls, the tabletops, or any flat surface in the entire home.

This couple was terrified of losing their possessions. After prolonged discussions, they agreed to have their possessions professionally appraised, catalogued, and videotaped for inventory and insurance purposes. I heard a story about each and every "treasure." We went over every item on their to-do list until they were satisfied. All of the papers required were handled by a proper professional, and all legal papers were eventually in order. They could now discuss with everyone who was to get what when they passed on. It was a long process, but in the end, they were very comforted, since we covered every detail that they could think of.

Many of us want to put our heads in the sand when it comes to legal issues, but that's how you get burned. Face things and solve issues now so your elder can better enjoy his or her remaining time, and so you can be more at ease in your caregiving role. Once everything is put in order, review all legal issues every five years, or more frequently if your elder has a particularly complicated situation.

Before you ever take your elder to a lawyer or other professional, write down your goals and objectives. Don't use a lawyer as a think tank. Perform your due diligence before you walk into the office. Prepare a list of questions if needed, and don't air your dirty laundry in front of an attorney. It only wastes time, brands you as a problematic client, and costs your elder money.

Understanding how you can be of assistance in meeting your elder's legal needs goes back to good communication. You must ask your elder the serious, tough questions about what he or she wants and needs. Then, proceed accordingly. Take care of what the senior desires, not what you desire. Something I've observed often is that the older generation bows more regularly to authority. The Baby Boomers play a different game, bending authority to their will. So often there's a clash of values and strategies played out with legal issues.

Step 6: Take Care of Legal Matters

Tread carefully here, as you should not impose your value system. After all, this isn't about you.

After going over financial and insurance details, you must collect and keep your elder's legal papers in a safe spot such as a lock box, safety deposit box, or fireproof safe. Petty cash can also be placed there. Legal papers commonly include the following documents, and there may be others as well:

- Birth certificate
- Marriage certificate(s)
- Divorce decree(s)
- Social Security card
- Military records (including discharge papers)
- Naturalization records
- Tax records
- Living will
- Health care power of attorney
- Health insurance policies and claims
- Medicare card and records
- Medicaid card and records
- Disability insurance policy
- Will
- Life insurance policy
- Funeral insurance policy
- Funeral instructions
- Cemetery plot deed
- Durable power of attorney
- Home deed and title
- Mortgage(s)
- Apartment lease
- Car title(s)
- Car insurance policy
- Homeowner's insurance policy
- Appraisals/valuations of collections including coins, jewelry, art

- Employment records
- Higher education diploma(s)
- "Do not resuscitate" order (DNR)
- Adoption papers
- Passport(s)

Protect your loved one by getting all in order expeditiously. Remember that every case is unique. There is no cookie-cutter formula to this process, but I've learned some tricks over my years as a geriatric care manager. Guess how many of my clients have everything in order before I come on board? A mere 30 percent! There are many questions to be answered, but the moment I begin with a client, I quickly focus on the issues listed below. Follow my lead, and you will be on your way to easing many legal problems. Again, I encourage you to hire a trusted lawyer, accountant, or tax professional if anything is unclear.

- Determine all of your elder's assets.
- Inventory all of your elder's valuable items.
- Take pictures and videotapes of all valuable items.
- If a valuable can fit in a pocket, move it out of the home and place it in storage or in a safe deposit box.
- Gather the legal documents listed earlier in this step.
- Execute a plan for your elder's estate.
- Open trusts if applicable.
- Assign power of attorney, which gives someone else the power to act on behalf of your elder. That person is legally responsible to act in your elder's best interest, but once in a while, this person abuses the power; so be careful who is selected.
- Assign durable power of attorney, which authorizes someone to act on behalf of your elder if he or she becomes unable to make his or her own decisions. It differs from power of attorney in that it can be enforced even if the person becomes disabled, so abuse is more common due to the greater power transfer. Use caution!

- Record exact instructions for the handling of your elder's remains. Some families have members with different belief systems, and complications often arise when last wishes are not in written form.

- Execute "do not resuscitate" (DNR) orders if so desired.

- Name someone as your elder's beneficiary, or his or her estate will be left to the state. Sadly, I've seen this happen many times, and family members can do little except deal with their shock.

- Hire an executor for the will if there is nobody in that role. Often, the executor of a will has retired or died or moved or sold his business.

- Are there "adopted" children who haven't been legally adopted? They will not enjoy inheritance rights unless the latter have been legally specified.

Very important: Don't place legal documents that need to be accessible twenty-four hours a day in a safe deposit box. I've had many clients do this and then be inconvenienced on the weekend or late at night when the bank is closed. Banks are immediately informed of someone's death. Safety deposit boxes are locked immediately upon a death notice. Without a certified death certificate you may not have immediate access.

Hospital Stays

If your elder ends up in a hospital, there's a new set of legal issues to consider. Be sure to read the patient's bill of rights at the hospital or other institution. The institution is required by law to provide you with it. Your elder is entitled to a certain level of care, and you should speak up if you feel that the hospital has not lived up to that standard. Many seniors have been conditioned to believe doctors are infallible, so they never question what's being done. This can mean it's up to you to closely monitor the level of care being provided.

Ask the hard questions, get access to information, and be involved in the care of your elder in order to have some control over what's being done to his or her body and mind. If he or she is sharing a room, be sure the roommates are socially appropriate. Is a comatose patient in the same room as a sex offender? Your elder needs privacy. Does the staff knock on the door? Is your elder washed and changed on time? Is there a locked place where he or she can store valuables or private items? Unfortunately, many seniors are victims of crime in health care facilities. Is there a receipt for items that the security department has locked away? Make sure that what your elder carries into a facility is recorded and returned upon departure or discharge.

The best way to be sure that your elder receives quality care is to enlist the help of the aides, orderlies, and nurses at the facility. Hospitals are small villages. When someone sneezes in the basement, they say, "God bless you" in the attic. If something is amiss, someone on staff will know—but don't approach him or her in an accusatory manner. Let the staff know you're involved and concerned and would like to be contacted if anything is amiss. Just as elsewhere in life, relationships are the key, so foster them from the moment your elder checks into any facility.

When in serious fear for your loved one's safety, contact local police, protective services, social workers, family counselors, or a hospital social worker. At a nursing facility, contact the head nurse for that particular floor, or the director of nursing, or the social worker assigned to your loved one.

HIPAA

The Health Insurance Portability and Accountability Act (HIPAA) is an important federal law that protects the privacy of senior citizens by defining who has legal access to their confidential medical information. Basically, it attempts to keep both professional and nonprofessional individuals from gaining access to your elder's medical information, or discriminating against them if they are legally privy to the medical records.

The wrong person reading your elder's file can now lead to big fines and even jail time for that person. Your elder cannot be barred from access to quality health care based on his or her specific situation. The law requires a designated representative who can access the files. Most hospitals and other health professionals will deal with one and only one "spokesperson" regarding your elder's medical treatment and records. Usually, this one person is the elder's spouse, the primary caregiver (you), or the health care proxy designee. If your elder is an *alleged incapacitated person (AIP)*, a court can assign guardianship of your elder to another individual, and that person will have access to your elder's medical records, but not you or your family. This is something you want to manage and control by putting it in writing before it gets to that stage.

The situation can become messy if your elder has not designated one person to have access to his or her records. Sometimes family members disagree about specific treatment options, or even refuse to be in the same room together due to bad blood, divorce, other wives/husbands, and the like. Hospital ethics committees and lawyers then get involved and it can become very sad. That's why I suggest that your elder name a HIPAA designee ahead of time if possible. This should be declared in a simple sentence in your elder's will, health care proxy, durable power of attorney, and DNR ("do not resuscitate" order).

Use HIPAA to your elder's advantage if you believe something illegal has occurred. The law can be quite confusing at times, but it's definitely making those in the medical profession more cautious about who gains access to a patient's medical information—and that's a good thing.

Guardianship

Caregivers should never take away the dignity, pride, or independence of a loved one, but you must always protect those who cannot protect themselves. Legal guardianship deals with the needs of an alleged incapacitated person (AIP). The system, managed by the courts, is set up to protect your elder. Can he or she still make sound judgments? If not, guardianship might be considered. The courts must protect an individual who is unable to take care of him or herself, and guardianship is an effective solution if your elder is in this state and, for whatever reason, you're unable to perform your caregiving role. It's also implemented in the event that a senior lacks family, friends, or a personal support system.

The court will assign professionals to evaluate your elder, and then come to a consensus on how to best protect him or her. Often, the AIP is put under the guardianship of the courts so that the assets, physical person, and rights are protected. The

Legal Terms to Know

Will: a legal document that states your intentions and what you wish to be done regarding disposal of your property after your death.

Advance directive: a legal statement signed by you, as a living, competent person, that expresses your wishes in advance of an emergency that makes you otherwise unable to convey your decisions. A living will is a type of advance directive.

Living will: a written document detailing the health care you want to receive if you are unable to speak for yourself because of medical incapacitation.

Health care proxy: a legal document in which you designate another person to make health care decisions for you if you are rendered incapable of making your wishes known. Also known as medical power of attorney.

Durable power of attorney: a power of attorney is a legal document that assigns legal authority to another person so he or she can make property, financial, and other legal decisions for you if you are unable to do so for yourself. In some states, health care decisions can be added to the responsibilities of the durable power of attorney.

Durable power of attorney for health care: a document allowing another or others to make health care decisions when you are not able to. Authorized by state law, this document allows you to designate another person to have powers, which you specify in the document. These powers can be limited to health care decisions, or for general financial management, health and medical care, and emergencies. This document can be revoked by you, as the principal, at any time if you remain competent.

guardian can be you, a local lawyer, a health care professional, a friend, or other family member. The guardian has the power to take care of your elder's needs.

I've seen this system work many times. It's usually implemented to save an elder who is being taken advantage of—someone who has limited ability to handle the end of his or her life and has nowhere else to turn for help. The entire process can be time-consuming, but it does protect people from predators. Guardianship guarantees that your elder will be looked after in his or her time of need.

One day my client, who was under my legal guardianship, had to go to the emergency room. She was disoriented and distraught because she did not know where she was. She could not understand why she was not at home. Because she had resources, I quickly hired the aide whom she had employed for years. This aide sat with her in the hospital, and the familiar, friendly face helped my client stay calm. The doctors didn't think she would live long. My client had one granddaughter, who lived a great distance away. She couldn't take on the responsibility of guardianship, but she loved her grandmother, so she came in for a short visit during the hospital stay. The granddaughter was grateful that her grandmother was being taken care of so well. She was able to provide additional background information as to who needed to be notified in the event that her grandmother passed on. There were very few relatives in this family, and all were older than her grandmother. All legal papers for this client had been in order for many years, and when she passed on, there was an easy transition of all legal issues.

Last Will and Testament

Do not allow your elder to die *intestate,* the legal term for dying without a will in place. When your elder doesn't have a will, the state takes over all of the assets. It can become very complicated, and you're sure to lose a hefty percentage of the true value of the estate. By making a will and assigning power of attorney, an elder will feel comforted that his or her wishes will be carried out.

Wills are often changed, so be ready to execute more than one document over time. I had one client, a woman in her late seventies, who crossed out every deceased person in her will. Nine of them were eventually excised—so many that four new wills had to be drawn up. And remember, anytime someone signs a will, there must be a witness. The original should be kept with the lawyer, and a copy should be included with your elder's other legal documents.

Complications also arise when a second family or step-family is involved. All variables should be well thought out, such as who is included and who is not included in the will. One way to leave someone out of a will is to give them exactly one dollar. This way, they can't contest the will and argue they were overlooked or that your elder was incompetent; a plan was put in place to include them. I've seen disputes of this sort happen far too frequently. Anyone who contests a will can hold up the process for years, even if that person has no legal ground to stand on.

It's very important to appoint the right person as executor or executrix of the will. Your elder must have confidence that he or she will carry out the full instructions of the will. This is one reason a guardian is usually a family member, a trusted family friend, or a lawyer.

Finally, don't draft your elder's will yourself or allow him or her to do it. If a will is not prepared in accordance with state laws, it could easily be challenged by other heirs and family members who are unhappy with its contents. This leaves the estate open to hefty legal fees and prolonged, ugly maneuvers that could have easily been avoided.

Step 7

Find Mobility in Disability

When our wheelchair-confined parents wanted to attend our son's wedding, we arranged an 800-mile trip for them. They each said the event was a highlight of their life.
—R.T., in Kansas

The ability to move around at will is the most basic manifestation of personal freedom. But now it's very likely that for the first time ever your elder is having difficulty leaving home. He or she might not be able to get around without the assistance of a walker, a cane, or a wheelchair. Driving may not be possible anymore. These newfound restrictions on mobility can have a devastating effect on your elder's psyche. It makes some elders feel as if they're in jail. As a caregiver, you have the job of smoothing the transition, and I encourage you to make your loved one feel independent no matter what struggles are encountered.

If your elder suffers from a disability that hampers the ability to walk or stand for long periods of time, then assisting his or her travel outside of the home is probably the most difficult task you'll face as a caregiver. You cannot imagine the difficulties associated with the situation until you experience them, but there are ways to make the most of it.

Start by taking advantage of what does work for your elder. If a wheelchair is required, you should become an expert wheelchair handler. Put yourself in the wheelchair and imagine what it would be like. If a limb is not fully functional, ask your loved one's doctor if therapy could improve its function and, if so, start him or her on a program. Take the approach that you're going to make the best of the situation, and your attitude will go a long way toward keeping your elder as mobile as possible.

Handicapped Access

Recent laws and the subsequent retrofitting of buildings have changed handicap access dramatically. When outside the home, be sure to take advantage of any handicap-friendly accommodations. These include parking spots, toilet facilities, wheelchair exits and entrances, adapted seating in restaurants and movie theaters, and the like. If your elder is still driving and is eligible for handicap parking privileges, make sure the doctor signs off on the proper paperwork for a department of motor vehicles pass. If your elder needs it, call ahead to determine what specific access is available at a given location. Find out if there are steps to navigate where you're going. I often purchase movie tickets ahead of time so my clients don't have to wait in line for tickets. When going to a doctor's office, prepare the wheelchair, paperwork, list of questions, medications, and so on the night before to ensure a smoother journey.

If your elder has special Department of Motor Vehicle handicap parking privileges, check ahead to see if parking is in the front of a building but the entrance is in the back. Count the number of steps from the car door to the front door of the establishment. Determine the location of the bathroom and whether it's handicap accessible. Is there a mirror your elder can look into in the bathroom? Is the sink wheelchair accessible? All of these variables should be taken into consideration.

Driving

More than any other activity, driving is directly linked to a senior citizen's independence. It takes one back to the days of youth and freedom. But driving privileges must be discussed if your elder is driving erratically or exhibiting poor judgment that can put his or her life or the lives of others in danger. Driving difficulties usually stem from your elder's physical deterioration, poor vision, reduced hearing, decreased ability to concentrate, and improper usage of medication.

Even if your elder is still competent behind the wheel, consider having him or her retested at the department of motor vehicles. There might be new laws that your elder needs to know. You can also make it more comfortable for your elder to drive. Here are ten steps to take:

- Make clear maps and put them in plastic so that they are stationary and easy to read.
- Limit radio use.
- Instruct your elder to dial or answer a cell phone only when the car is parked. You also have the option of enabling "Do Not Disturb While Driving" mode.
- Be sure the car is clean, full of gas, and in good working order.
- Be sure the windows are clean inside and out, and the windshield wipers are in top working condition.
- Recommend a defensive driving class to learn any new laws and safety techniques.
- Make sure the driver is never under the influence of alcohol or medication that impairs reaction time, hearing, or vision or that causes drowsiness.
- Subscribe to a roadside service in case of emergency.
- Be sure the car insurance is up to date.
- Keep a list of emergency phone numbers in the glove compartment or in the driver's wallet or purse.

Also take a hard look at whether or not your elder should still be operating a motor vehicle. Here are five important questions to consider:

- Is your elder a competent driver during the day, but incompetent at night?
- Does your elder see 20/20 with corrective lenses, but has drastically reduced peripheral vision?
- Does your elder do well driving locally but struggles at higher speeds or when directions are needed?
- Is your elder hitting curbs, missing turns, or putting pedestrians at risk?

• Has your elder been in an accident that was deemed his or her fault?

If you can answer yes to just one of these questions, it could be time to take your elder off the road. Determine whether or not there's a way to correct his or her vision or enhance concentration behind the wheel. Take your elder to the department of motor vehicles for an eye test and a basic road test. If he or she passes, you might be able to get special handicapped driving privileges.

Handicapped License

A handicapped license is a more permanent solution and comes with a sticker or tag for your elder's car windshield or license plate. It allows your elder to park in the handicapped parking places, which are usually closer to the front door. If the difficult situation will soon pass, you may just need to get a doctor's note to have handicapped privileges granted for a short period of time. This is different from a handicapped license and expires when the condition improves. Both the license and the temporary sticker or tag will allow your elder to park in handicapped spaces.

When it's time for license renewal, if your elder doesn't pass the driving test, present him or her with the failed test result. But don't just take the keys away. Be sensitive about the situation and plan how you're going to take the keys away. Involve your elder in the process: If the car is no longer needed, sell it and put the money toward a transportation budget. Always look for creative solutions. Open an account with a taxi service such as Uber or Lyft, or find a transportation service for the elderly.

When my own father was aging, I became his geriatric care manager. Though I had years of experience, I still found it difficult to make all of the required adjustments to care for him. Because my father lived out of state, I ended up on a plane too often because people in the field did not always answer phone calls or e-mail messages. I had to do many things that required me to be there in person.

The hardest transition was when my father could no longer drive. We talked through the problem and the possibility of him injuring himself or others. We ceremoniously hung up the car keys, and notified the department of motor vehicles and his car insurance company. We sold the car and turned in his license plates. Then I bought my father an adult tricycle with two baskets (one in front, the other in back) for his short trips to the grocery store. He put his toy poodle in the front basket and his groceries in the other. The bike gave him transportation, exercise, and fresh air. The end result was that he started to meet more people because he was out and about and more visible. I also arranged for a bus service and taxi service to take him to events.

Having driving privileges revoked could cause a host of problems for your elder, such as the loss of the primary source of transportation, reduced social status, and the inability to easily purchase food and bring it home. Your loved one could find it difficult to attend social gatherings or help friends in need. Loss of the privilege could also increase his or her anxiety level due to both real and imagined isolation, which should be avoided at all costs. Encourage family and friends to visit, schedule the weekly card game to take place in your elder's house, and determine new ways to bring entertainment into the home.

Other Transportation

Because giving up driving can be traumatic and greatly impact your elder's daily life, other modes of transportation need to be investigated and utilized. These include public transportation, private limousines, taxis, car services, and carpooling. If such modes of transportation are available in your town, show your elder how to use the subway, the bus, and/or the train. Public transportation also has senior discounts. Many communities provide transportation for the elderly; these include senior centers, community centers, and religious groups. It may take some digging to find the resources, but it's worth the effort to keep your elder moving about if at all possible. This is especially important because he or she might feel frightened due to diminishing capacities. A sedentary person declines dramatically faster than one who still leads an active lifestyle. Some metropolitan areas have Access A Ride transportation as well.

Wheelchairs

A few years ago, I had a fresh-faced batch of geriatric care management students in my program. I made their first training mission a real doozie. They had to spend an entire day in a wheelchair, and try to get around town as if it were a regular day. They had to get to my class, try to make a phone call from a pay phone, get in and out of an elevator, use a public restroom, eat at a restaurant, shop in a convenience store, and so on. That mission woke them up to the realities of a wheelchair-bound life. I suggest you do the same so that you have a real understanding of what one goes through when adapting to a wheelchair-centric existence.

Your elder's wheelchair could be the only effective way of getting around, so you should treat it like a favorite car or other prized possession. The more time and effort you spend on it, the longer the wheelchair will last and the better it will perform, making your role as a caregiver far easier. As with a car, preventive maintenance is the key and should reduce the amount of time and money you spend at the wheelchair repair shop. Make it a habit to clean the wheelchair; wipe off spills the moment they occur, and they will occur often. This prevents movable joints from becoming caked with debris. Also, clean and disinfect seat upholstery on a weekly basis, especially if your elder is incontinent. Regularly inspect the tires and spokes, and remove any items that have become stuck to the tires, such as gum, strings, wrappers, and food.

Be on the lookout for these common wheelchair hazards:

- Defective locks and brakes
- Broken or poorly adjusted front rigging
- Poorly aligned and/or loose wheels
- Broken or malfunctioning seat belt
- Broken hand rims that have loose screws or chipped chrome
- Ripped or badly worn upholstery
- Broken spokes or skirt guards

The Wheelchair

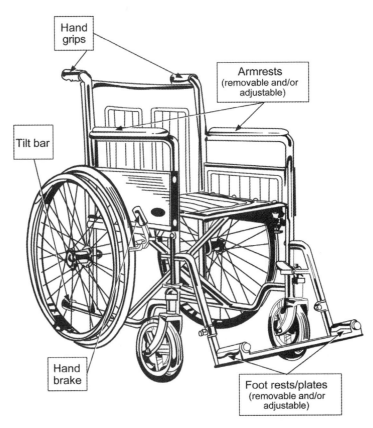

Hand grips

Armrests
(removable and/or adjustable)

Tilt bar

Hand brake

Foot rests/plates
(removable and/or adjustable)

- Wax build-up on wheels and casters

Safety is also an important issue for wheelchairs. Seat belts should be fastened at all times. Many don't realize it, but it's the law—just as it is for cars. Wheel locks and brakes should always be engaged before your elder gets in or out of the wheelchair. Make sure he or she is seated properly in the wheelchair, not tilted to the side, front, or back. Feet should rest comfortably on the foot plate, not hang or drag on the floor. Your elder's arms should also be inside the armrests or on the lap, not hanging to the side.

Before transporting your elder, you should become an expert at using hand grips and push handles to climb up and descend from curbs, and to get in and out of elevators. Watch out for common hazards such as uneven floors, cracks in the ground or in sidewalks, and gaping holes in pavement. Wet floors, automatic doors, and elevators are also dangerous.

When it comes to ease of moving in a wheelchair, I have a few pet peeves. Handicapped-accessible locations are often anything but. I usually have to go around to the back of business entrances to ring a bell, and it's very frustrating when nobody answers the door. It's also an issue when people who don't need special treatment park in handicapped parking spots. The latter often occurs in the winter when snowplows pile snow so high that it blocks handicapped entrances to parking lots or buildings. Watch out for all of these problems because you want to eliminate any hassles that might impact your elder.

Electronic Sleep Equipment

Continuous positive airway pressure (CPAP) therapy is the leading form of treatment for *obstructive sleep apnea (OSA)*. Before one can begin CPAP therapy, the disorder must first be diagnosed through a sleep study to determine the existence and severity of OSA. Once a determination of OSA has been made and CPAP therapy has been established as the recommended treatment, a prescription for a CPAP machine must be obtained before equipment can be issued.

Under federal law, medical devices are categorized into three classes—class I, II, or III—based on their risks and the regulatory controls necessary to provide a reasonable assurance of safety and effectiveness by the Food and Drug Administration (FDA).

Who can write CPAP prescriptions?

- Medical doctors
- Doctor of osteopathy
- Psychiatrist (M.D. only)
- Physician assistant
- Nurse practitioner
- Dentist
- Naturopathic physicians

Insurances require a prescription to cover payments.

Without a prescription, they will not pay for equipment. Prescriptions come with a set pressure setting based on results of the sleep study. A machine cannot be adequately set without pressure settings. Pressure settings should only ever be determined by a board-certified sleep specialist's interpretation of the sleep study.

Long-Distance Travel

Aging does not necessarily prevent your elder from traveling or interacting with the world at large if he or she has the capacity, drive, and perseverance to do so. Travel can still be an exciting experience, but it takes a great deal of organization. State bureaus of tourism, state parks, historical societies, and local chambers of commerce are all excellent sources of travel information, but you must be very specific regarding any special needs your loved one might have. The more specific you are, the more accurate the information you will receive. A bed and breakfast will often have a room that can accommodate a special needs person, including wheelchair-accessible shower stalls. Always check for senior and/or handicapped discounts and consider traveling midweek or off-season. You can also ask for a discount for yourself or an aide if finances are an issue.

It's also quite common for your elder to be invited to family gatherings or special events. This can be both a joy and a challenge, especially if the event is at a distance. One of my clients was invited to a wedding, a surprise birthday for her sister three months later, and a gathering of "the clan" for a family reunion six months after that. These invitations produced a lot of anxiety for her, and meant a lot of detail work on my part for her to enjoy a stress-free time with family and friends.

After discussing every possible detail together, we made lists for each event—all supplies, medications, other items that would be needed, and what had to be purchased, such as new outfits or gifts. Gifts were always sent in advance, even if they were checks. I checked out the transportation and the hotels, and her aide went with her to all three events. She took a plane on one trip and a train to the others. Everything went as planned, and I asked family members at each event to supply us with pictures. When the pictures arrived, they were enjoyed and then put into a scrapbook. This gave her another chance to discuss and show all her friends each of the various events.

Traveling with your elder can be exponentially more complicated than traveling alone. Complications you would never think of can arise, so plan ahead. Something as simple as jetlag could pose a major problem, as it takes seniors twice as long to recover; so you have to factor that in. Because most caregivers are very focused on what's going on in their own lives, I've compiled a list of special considerations when traveling long distances with your elder.

- If staying in a hotel, check to see if there are specially equipped handicap rooms available that have wide doors for wheelchair access and a special bathroom and shower.

- If your elder requires oxygen, a medical note from the doctor should accompany you at all times, detailing how much oxygen is needed and how often it must be refilled.

- If your loved one is taking other medication, always carry a full set of written prescriptions with you, especially if needles are required. The police can stop you. It has happened to me before.

- Carry a second set of eyeglasses and your elder's prescription in case you lose the primary pair.

- Most hotels offer a reduced rate for seniors. Take advantage of it.

- If you'll need a stretcher to transport your elder, arrange for one in advance.

- There's often a quota on how many wheelchairs can be accommodated on planes, buses, and trains. Be sure your elder is included before the maximum is reached.

- If your elder is a quadriplegic, arrange ahead of time for special seating that's closer to the door or bathroom.

- If your elder is blind, alert the airlines about a seeing-eye dog, if appropriate. Also let the hotel know.

- If your elder is traveling alone, get the name of a flight attendant or train conductor who can supervise until someone meets him or her at the other end. I've also hired nurses to meet especially frail clients at the other end.

- Pay extra for nonstop flights, trains, and buses to reduce travel time and other complications, such as changing planes.

- Think of your elder's dietary needs. He or she should carry a double supply of food in case of an unscheduled delay.

- Pack everything as if you're in the Army (crisp folds and rolls). Clothing ends up less wrinkled, and more will fit in the luggage.

- Make sure all luggage is tagged with distinct identification (such as a piece of tape or a bow) since a lot of luggage looks the same.

- If your elder has other special needs, write down everything and give it to the airline attendant or train conductor. This includes medical requirements, dietary concerns, sleep aids, special clothing, adapted equipment, and emergency phone numbers, plus name and address and trip itinerary.

- If you're traveling as well, it's your job to bring all emergency equipment with you, such as medication, prescriptions, and so forth. Don't put them in your baggage because it could be lost.

- Keep your elder's passport on his or her person at all times.

- Exchange currency before your elder arrives in the foreign country to avoid long lines or confusion at the destination.

- If traveling to another country, buy as much of what your elder needs as possible in the United States.

- Some rental car agencies have cars that are adapted for wheelchairs and other handicapped issues, so call ahead and book this service if required.

- If your elder leaves town on short notice, be sure someone is told where he or she is going.
- If a problem arises, you must be able to locate him or her in a hurry. I recommend that my clients wear an identification bracelet or necklace at all times.

Traveling Alone on an Airline

There are many things you can do to smooth airline travel for your elder. One wheelchair is allowed on board most flights, so call ahead to check if your elder can bring his or her own wheelchair on board if necessary. Wheelchairs and other mobility devices may also be checked at the gate. These special checked items can then be made available to the elder at the end of the flight as they disembark. Also, seniors traveling alone who need assistance between airport gates or with luggage can request help ahead of time. Make sure the airline personnel are aware that your elder is traveling with them before you arrive at the airport.

Be aware that airline and airport regulations are constantly changing and being updated. It is important when making reservations and accommodations that every flight detail is worked out for all departures and arrivals. Check and double check every aspect of the itinerary, especially if the airline will be handling any adaptive equipment.

Clothing for Travel

An important variable that affects your elder's mobility is clothing. Make sure he or she always has the proper attire. Improper clothing can often restrict your elder's movements, so be sensitive to this. Clothing shouldn't be torn or too tight or too loose. When the wearer is sitting down, the clothing waistline should be flexible and not binding. If a man has a tough time keeping his pants up, sew little buttons on the inside or have him wear suspenders. Many elderly require several layers of clothing, especially in the winter, so plan accordingly.

If your elder has a bandage that's covering a healing wound, you must provide nonbinding clothes, not just pajamas. The latter may look sloppy and take away one's dignity. I'm a big believer in Velcro because it provides more flexibility and room. For instance, you can use it on a man's fly if he does not have the finger dexterity to deal with zippers or buttons. If incontinency is part of the equation, let out the pants seam so that there is less pressure on the bladder. Your elder still wants to look good. You should keep his or her dignity intact and allow as much mobility and fun as possible in the later years. Your elder can still go to the wedding, christening, or bar mitzvah and not bring unwanted attention in the process.

If there are motor control issues, I teach my clients how to put on their own socks again, if only to maintain a slice of independence. I show them how to grasp one pant leg to raise that leg across the other leg so that it's easier to put on socks. I also suggest that they buy shoes that have Velcro straps instead of laces so that it's easier to slip shoes on and off. Also, for men who wear a tie, they should just loosen the tie when finished wearing it, rather than undoing it all the way, so there's no need to tie it from the start the next time.

Finally, be sure your elder has a long hanging mirror in the home. Seniors should always be able to check out their appearance before leaving the home. You'd be surprised at how many no longer have mirrors in their living environment.

Step 8

Find the Right Housing

*When my parents decided to move closer to us, we
helped find appropriate accommodations to meet their needs.
We also supervised the move out of their apartment, made
transportation arrangements, and then helped them move
across five states. They told us it made a big difference as they
left their familiar surroundings and home of forty years.*
—B.D., in New York

You're probably reading this step because something
about your loved one's living environment is
inappropriate. Perhaps he or she is forced to share space, live
in a rundown home, or live with a relative or a friend. Maybe
the place is too dirty or unsafe. Perhaps the neighborhood has
changed, or there's a leaky roof, or the amount of care required
has increased. Regardless, it has drawn your attention and
you have to make significant changes to improve your elder's
quality of life. You know the environment must be improved
to keep your elder safe, healthy, and at ease.

One of my clients lived in the same small apartment
for forty-seven years. He had forty years worth of articles
stacked up for supposed "research." But he wasn't a writer or
researcher, and I doubt that he had looked at the articles again
since the day he saved them. We wanted to move him, but he
was adamant about staying put. He said, "I know this place
is dirty, Doctor Marion, but it's my dirt! I know where every
bit of it came from. If you throw it away, you'll be throwing
me away." I couldn't do that, so I brought in a professional

organizer. With my client's input, three weeks later the place was in order. He lived there in peace for another seven years until he passed away.

According to the AARP, 24 percent of Baby Boomers expect their parents or in-laws to move in with them. It's estimated that nearly half of all American families are caring for both elderly parents and young children.

Another time, I was hired by a family that was very involved with their two elderly aunts, and each one needed a different level of care. The family and the two aunts wanted to continue to live together in their family home, but it was becoming increasingly difficult to manage the situation. One aunt was now in a wheelchair and the other was using a walker. They didn't want to leave their home, and each had a variety of other ailments and different medical needs. After much discussion with all concerned parties, we hired an architect, who made the interior of the home wheelchair accessible. We also made the front and garden entrances wheelchair accessible so that it was easier for the sisters to move through the home.

At first, the family balked at the cost of the changes, and they didn't want to deal with the noise and mess of the construction. But once the financial costs of institutional placement and the emotional toll of the change of environment were added up, it was clear what had to be done. Ultimately, this project brought incredible harmony to the entire family. The sisters also used this time together to investigate assisted living and the local nursing facility so that they were aware of their options if a higher level of care was ever needed in the future. After all of the improvements were completed, the sisters were able to stay in their own home for another six years, which gave me a deep sense of satisfaction.

Caregiving is a lot like sailing: You have to set a goal and keep your eye on it, even if it means tacking back and forth along unexpected paths to reach your destination. This is especially true of your elder's living arrangements. During the course of your caregiving journey, your loved one might have two, three, or even four different places of residence. It's up to you to calmly guide the process.

Many people erroneously believe that the majority of the elderly population ends up in a nursing facility soon after the first signs of dramatic decline. In fact, only roughly 5 percent of the elderly population requires skilled nursing care. So, what should you do? Carefully consider all of your options when choosing living arrangements.

There are several basic choices for your elder:

- Live alone in the current home.
- Live in the home with an aide or hired help and/or adapted equipment.
- Move in with you or another friend or relative.
- Move to a retirement home
- Move to a continuity of care campus
- Move to an assisted living facility.
- Move to a nursing facility.
- Move to hospice care or have in-home hospice care.

After I'm hired by a family, I talk to the elder and get the real story about what's going on. You have to get the following facts: How is the senior's health? Is he or she safe? Are basic needs being met in regard to care, nutrition, and medications? Truth be told, it's rare that you'll have to make radical changes immediately, even though it might seem like it. Ask your elder's opinion of the options and the living situation. Find out how much information the senior has. Most of all, what effect does the current housing situation have on his or her health and happiness?

Do you want to move your elder? If so, you must consider his or her needs and focus on the right option. Most elderly want to remain in their familiar environment until they absolutely have to leave, so it's usually easier on both of you if you fix and improve the current environment. If your loved one is moved from one home or hospital to another, there is often a transfer trauma. Everything familiar changes and it takes time for your elder to adjust. Take into account such things as the orientation and the new environment, as well as the sounds, smells, and food. It usually takes a while to get used to it, especially for someone who is nonverbal. Just moving to a room with a window in the same facility or institution requires an adjustment period. So, give your elder that time and space to adjust.

Also consider whether the elder can self-medicate or if help is required for dispensing medication. Is his or her food delivered or cooked? Can he or she eat alone? How does your elder currently get to the doctor? What are the specific health issues, and can they be managed if your elder lives alone? Are you considering moving your elder because it's best for him or her or best for you? Be honest! Try to think of all of the physical, emotional, financial, and psychological issues that are involved. Have a realistic evaluation done for everyone's sake.

Perhaps you're dealing with guilt, frustration, and anger over care and housing issues. A good way to alleviate this is to perform all of the safety checks in Step 2: Put Safety First. Fix everything that you can to allow your elder to live at home. Add adapted equipment if it will improve the situation. Teach your elder how to use adapted equipment or new appliances. Don't take him or her out of the home until it is a clear "best option."

Also, hiring an aide can ease your senior's condition and extend his or her time in the home. Another popular choice is hiring coordinated services to assist with and care for your elder. This also allows seniors to live at home longer than they would otherwise. These services include employing an aide in the home for a set number of hours per day, employing a visiting nurse to administer medications on a weekly basis, and hiring an aide to coordinate meal delivery. Your support system of family and friends can play a significant role here. If your elder has been doctor diagnosed with a specific, limited time to live, hospice is an option to consider as well.

Keeping Your Elder at Home

Below are reasons why you should strive to allow your elder to remain in the home at all costs.

- It's more affordable. The average nursing facility now costs $55,000 to $100,000 plus a year. Keeping your elder at home should cost much less than that.

- Familiar surroundings make your loved one feel calm and centered.

- Neighbors can help you keep an eye on your elder.

- Your elder has many positive, cherished memories in his or her home. Some argue that removing your elder from the home breaks the cycle of life.

- The smells, the furniture, and the kitchen are all familiar. Moving to a sterile place that smells like plastic and medication can send your elder into a prolonged period of depression that drains precious energy.

- You can take a loan or mortgage against the home's equity.

- You can take a reverse mortgage if your elder is short on available cash.

If your elder is absolutely unable to remain in the home environment, the next logical step is to decide when to move him or her. Determine constraints and the network of family and friends who might be able to house your elder. One important suggestion: Never separate a couple unless it's necessary. I've seen so many instances where that very choice makes both people unhappy the rest of their living days. Couples who have been together for fifty years would rather be dead than separated, even if they've argued a lot. Whom else would they spar with?

A Word about Construction

If you make changes in an apartment, co-op, condominium, or home, you need to be aware of the rules governing each of these environments. There may be specific construction permits and guidelines to follow or specific contractors to hire. It's better to gain all of the necessary details and approvals rather than have to rip out the new construction and start all over again.

After doing due diligence on one of my client's apartments, we made substantial changes because he was a wheelchair-confined paraplegic. We lowered the kitchen cabinets, changed the door knobs so that they were easier to turn, and then removed many of the apartment doors. We also widened the doorways, put tilted mirrors in the bathroom and bedroom, and installed environmental control units so he could activate various controls from his wheelchair. He lived in this newly workable environment for several years, and when he needed to go to the hospital for his last days, he expressed gratitude for being able to remain independent during that time.

Moving

Moving your loved one is a much more complicated process than just moving yourself. First, you must take into account the emotional element of removing him or her from a place that's familiar and holds a lifetime's worth of memories. Second, you have to decide what possessions get moved and what is donated to friends, relatives, charity, or just discarded. If your loved one is competent to be a part of the decision-making process, he or she should be consulted at every step. Keep in mind that possessions and treasures should never be treated lightly. Proceed with caution, be clear with your questions and comments, and always remember that you're dealing with someone's emotions, as well as family and personal history.

Moving into Your Home

You could also move your elder into your home. In many cultures and societies, this is the tradition. Consider it strongly. It's best to keep your elder in a familiar, loving environment if he or she must be moved. Are you able to adapt your living space? Can you build an addition or retrofit some square footage in your home? Can your kids double up and give one of their rooms? Is the floor plan of your home flexible? This can be a very difficult setup, especially if your spouse never got along with your elder, but you should consider it, along with the impact on everyone concerned.

Beware that having another person in your home, especially your mother or father, carries a lot of emotional history. Avoid misunderstandings by facilitating open, clear communication with your family and your elder. Also, there are usually dietary issues to consider and medication that has to be monitored. This extra responsibility and change in your home and family structure can affect your family's sense of peace.

Does your elder have enough money to live the remaining days? More often than not, extra money from your pocket is required to support your elder. What services is your elder eligible for? This can help defray costs and provide much needed care. Don't make a move without a thorough discussion and understanding of the financial and legal ramifications.

If necessary, you can also increase your elder's ability to recognize rooms in the home. Put his or her name or photo on the bedroom door. Or put his or her favorite flower on the kitchen table. These are helpful cues that allow one to live more comfortably.

Moving into an Adult Home

An adult home is perfect for someone who still leads an independent life and would like to live with other seniors in a safe environment. This is an attractive option because other people who are your elder's age live there, and they often share common interests and histories. Your elder may have the chance to make new friends and companions. All of this helps maintain independence, and that should be strived for at all times. Three communal meals are served per day, and there is usually a personal living space such as your elder's own apartment.

If you choose this option, be sure to hold on to your loved one's home for at least three months or until you know he or she likes the new environment, the food, the care, and even the smell. You might need the apartment or home again because it often takes up to six months before your elder will feel comfortable in his or her new environment. Consider getting rid of your elder's old clothing and keepsakes. Don't pay to have it packed and held in storage, although you don't want to throw things away willy-nilly. I can't tell you how many times I've seen families just throw away old items that their elder has had in storage for years; so discuss with your elder what to keep and what to discard.

Moving into an Assisted Living Facility

Assisted living provides the next level of care. Aides are on site, and they're attuned to the needs of their geriatric population. Household chores are performed: Sheets are changed, laundry is done, and food is cooked and served. Some homes even have a beauty parlor on site. Grocery service is often available, too. These facilities are also very secure, and offer sign-in and sign-out privileges. The medical staff is usually on call twenty-four hours a day, and there are aides to watch for memory-impaired residents. Ask about all additional costs, as they can add up quickly.

Assisted living provides other important services for your elder. These include recreation activities and expeditions to events, malls, restaurants, and movies, as well as regular bus service and other transportation. There's often a waiting list to get into an assisted living facility, so be sure to ask when inquiring for your elder. It can be a great option, but it can be costly. A warning: Be careful of what agreements your elder signs upon moving in. These facilities have been known to add expensive charges for some services (such as laundry and transportation) that you might think are included in the monthly fee. Promises may not be fulfilled, so read the fine print. Use caution when signing the lease, because it's a legal document. Have your lawyer go over the contract and ask the right questions. It's not a simple lease, so make sure everything is understood before signing. By what percentage will rent rise over what period of time? Is the facility affiliated with a local nursing facility, hospital, or college? Has the facility been around for a while, and has it established a shining reputation?

Moving into a Nursing Facility

Nursing facilities are tailored for residents who require a significant amount of care. Seniors who are unable to function independently can benefit greatly from the mental, physical, and emotional services available on site. Residents used to live in nursing facilities for seven years on average. Today, residents live there for less than two years because they now arrive at a more advanced age and with a higher complexity of health problems. Nursing facilities are expensive, but could prove to be the perfect fit for your elder. Other good candidates for nursing facilities include elderly with advanced medical problems and impaired elderly who don't have family and friends living nearby. The nursing facility provides them with a vital new community and support system.

I once had a client who loved her longtime nanny from Harlem. As her nanny aged, my client wanted to take care of her in the best possible way, so we arranged for the nanny to join her in an upscale nursing facility in suburban Connecticut. We were surprised when the nanny didn't want to go. She said, "It's filled with too many rich folks, and I'm not a rich folk." So, we found a facility for the nanny in Brooklyn, and she happily stayed there until she passed away.

What do you need to know about nursing facilities? Visit the location. Take the tour. Contact an admissions person and be prepared to ask him or her important questions. Check out at least three facilities before you decide on the right fit for your elder. Each one has a different atmosphere. Trust your gut. Bring other siblings or your oldest children along to help with the decision. Make another visit to facilities you like at an unscheduled time. Look around and observe the little things. Get a sense of the place as it really is, not just as the staff wants you to see it on the tour. Bring your elder to the facility and make him or her a part of the decision-making process when possible. Watch and listen to other residents. Always get references. Check out the National Association of Nursing Homes for a list of nursing facilities in your local area.

Answer the following questions:

- Is security obvious and a priority?
- Are residents well dressed?
- Is the first-floor bathroom clean?
- How is the food in the cafeteria?
- Is the physical plant in top condition?
- Is the staff attentive to the residents' needs?
- Are residents clean and well behaved?
- Do residents seem content? Are any wandering the halls, looking lost?
- Are the wheelchairs clean and fully functional?
- Are the activities enjoyable and age-appropriate?

- Is appropriate music playing? (I can't tell you how often I walk into a nursing facility to find staffers blasting rock and roll music that the residents don't want to hear.)
- Is the communal TV tuned to elder-appropriate programming or the favorite show of on-duty staffers?
- Is the facility insured?
- Will you and your elder have access to staff members?
- Do staff members knock before entering residents' rooms?

Observe if communication occurs on an adult-to-adult basis between staff and residents. Have two choices ready to go in case you're put on the waiting list by the first choice. This is common at popular nursing facilities.

Make sure you read the contract carefully before your senior moves in. Know what your elder is signing and be aware of all charges. Promises may be misunderstood, so read the fine print. You should keep in mind all of the questions to ask regarding assisted living facilities, such as whether your elder is eligible for Medicaid and who will help process such papers.

After your elder is admitted, I strongly recommend you attend the family orientation, and then visit often. Attend periodic meetings with staff members so you better understand what's happening with your elder, both subtle and obvious. This can be a good time to thank the staff for their help and effort as well as an opportune moment to ask pressing questions or have your concerns addressed.

Hospice

Hospice is a specialized program of palliative care for patients and/or residents who have less than six months to live, though this requirement can vary from state to state. Hospice attempts to give the elder the best possible quality of life during the dying process. It's also designed to meet any special needs of the family and friends. The primary focus is to make the senior comfortable and pain-free through the use of pain management medications prescribed by a physician.

Hospice care can take place in a variety of environments, and many choose to host hospice care in their own homes or in a familiar hospital, assisted living space, or nursing facility. Hospice makes sure your elder is cared for, and it better prepares the family and everyone else for the coming death. It can be scheduled at specific times if that's the request of the individual and/or the family. Hospice can also provide social, spiritual, and psychological counseling for dying seniors and their family members.

I was once hired by a family when they learned their father had less than four months to live. They wanted to have care provided for him at home, so we hired a full-time aide for the day shift. In the evening, the family members took turns providing care. I had suggested hospice care, but the family was sure they could handle this on their own. There were a lot of helping hands and loving hearts. I ordered some adapted equipment to make the task easier. Unfortunately, the physical, emotional, and psychological demands quickly began to wear them down, even though they were high-energy, big-hearted people. Finally, after much discussion, the family allowed hospice to enter the environment. When their father died, the family members were united in strength and peace at his bedside. All family members were able to be with their father during his four-month journey, and each had an opportunity to say good-bye.

Step 9

Hire Help When It's Needed

My mother had a heart attack and needed considerable attention when she came home from the hospital. I coordinated the services of a registered nurse and a home care aide; then I helped my family again when my mother needed to go to a higher level of care. I had to think about my own needs as well as my mother's. I'm an only child, but with Doctor Marion's help, I never felt alone.

—S.Z., in Michigan

The caregiving challenge could be one of the most difficult things you face in your life. You can't go it alone. If at all possible, you should hire help when and where appropriate to take some of the caregiving load off of your shoulders. Trust me, you'll need a break, and this step shows you how to hire the right aide for your elder and for you.

It's often quite difficult, if not impossible, for your elder to find a trustworthy, affordable housekeeper, handy person, or aide. Seniors often don't know where to find the contacts or what the going rate is for services that are needed. Make your elder's life easier and safer by taking on this responsibility. Do research, ask your friends and your elder's friends for references, interview candidates, and then hire someone.

Hiring help or assistance can be time-consuming, but it's well worth the effort, and if you're persistent, you'll eventually find the right person. After I interview an aide, I also have my client speak with the person to make sure he or she feels comfortable. It's your elder's home and space, and he or she usually doesn't take too kindly to "outsiders."

I once had an especially hard time finding an aide for a client who suffered from severe mood swings. She had already fired several aides within an eight-week period. When the fifth aide was let go, I insisted we make a list of both the qualities she wanted in an aide and the qualities and expertise I thought were necessary. My list was long, but her list was longer! We matched up where we agreed, and then discussed the other issues until we were of one mind. When aides arrived to be interviewed, I didn't do any of the talking. She liked one applicant and hired her right away. That aide was with my client until she died several years later.

The first thing you must do is figure out exactly what kind of help you need. Often, your elder's needs (as well as your own) can be met by tapping into your network of family and friends. Look into this before you hire anyone. Ask who in this network is available to help. Don't be afraid to ask. As we discussed earlier, some family and friends can offer financial help, transportation, food, cooking skills, or legal expertise. Get as much free help as you can, but be clear about your elder's needs when asking friends and family for their assistance. How long will your loved one require their help—a few weeks, months, a year? People are more likely to lend a hand if the role and time commitment are both clearly defined. They like to know where the finish line is. Some will contribute to a short sprint, whereas others will be in it for the long haul. You have to know how to ask for help from all types.

The most common tasks include cleaning the home; handyman work such as fixing broken items, loose wires, windows, and rotted wood; and taking care of trash disposal. There's a wide variety of help available in your local community, so be resourceful about where and how you find the help. You can hire help on a daily, weekly, or monthly basis, all determined by your needs, your financial ability, and your elder's wishes. Search out community and government services as well as family aides and religious organizations.

As you consider hiring help, determine the answers to the following questions:

- Who is going to pay for the help (you/your elder/ insurance)?

- Does the helper take insurance as a form of payment? If so, what insurance?
- Should you hire a therapist and, if so, what type(s)?
- Does your elder need an aide or companion to live in the home 24/7?
- Who pours and dispenses your elder's medication?

Aides should be hired only to take care of your elder and perform the agreed-upon chores directly related to that care. Don't load them up with extraneous duties, even if you see that they're highly competent—unless, of course, the aide agrees to it. Then, they should be duly compensated for additional tasks. Also—and this is very important—take the time to make a match. Have the potential helper spend some time with your elder before he or she is hired.

For help in finding candidates, consult www.doctormarion. com for lists of agencies in your area that provide these services.

The Interview

After you have determined what sort of help is required, the next step is interviewing applicants. Always consider more than one candidate for the job; it's the best way to find a good match. Ask for references, and then check them. When interviewing prospects, ask the following questions:

- How long have you been in the field?
- What is your educational background?
- What professional organizations do you belong to?
- Are you insured?
- Are you bonded?
- Where have you worked previously?
- Do you charge hourly, daily, monthly, overall, or by the shift?
- Will you travel if required?
- Do you charge any possible hidden expenses or ongoing fees?
- Is there a less expensive monthly rate available?

- What are your strengths?
- What are your weaknesses?
- Do you understand the Medicare/Medicaid eligibility process?
- Is there a difference in cost between the day and the night shifts?
- Are you reliable and honest?
- Are you an expert in your discipline?
- What payment is expected for vacation, holidays, and sick days?

Experience is a huge factor. Determine if the aide has done this sort of work before, where, and for how long. Can the aide shave a man who can't hold up his head? Has the aide ever changed an adult diaper? Ask the tough questions so that you and your elder don't find yourselves in a terrible predicament because you were afraid to approach a sensitive subject. Be up front about salary, wages, holiday pay, taxes, and legal paperwork. If your elder has a live-in aide/companion, accommodate with sleeping arrangements. It's your responsibility. Don't employ undocumented workers, and don't abuse or overwork the aide.

Contract and Duties

Organize the sort of help you're considering into broad categories before you make any calls. Figure out what you and your elder want and need. These categories include feeding, bathing, the ability to facilitate your loved one's social life, and transportation. After interviewing candidates and hiring a helper, negotiate and sign a contract that explicitly states the terms of the agreement. You don't want any misunderstandings or ambiguities. Type up a clear list of duties to eliminate any confusion. The list should include timeframes for the work to be completed. If more than one aide has been hired, be sure to divide up the tasks according to specialty. Don't hire one person to do everything if he or she isn't competent in all fields. There are often local agencies that provide this type of help. Set good habits from the get-go, and don't let anyone take advantage of you, which will happen unless you set strict rules. Consider keeping a logbook of who is assigned to do what, and when that aide is supposed to complete the various tasks.

When I first started as a geriatric care manager, my clients often taught me about the best way to care for them. One client was happy with her aide but was forever fretting that the groceries were not exactly what she had included on her shopping list. I decided to go to the grocery store with the aide on her next outing. We walked up and down the aisles, and I designed my shopping list (*see* Appendix D: Logbooks) according to how the aide shopped. The list included the items that were usually purchased in each aisle as well as the brands that my client liked. This applied to everything: paper products, jams, meats, fish, fruits, vegetables, and anything else you can think of. From that moment on, shopping was no longer a point of contention between my client and her aide. My clients now use several pre-prepared lists that I update periodically as more items need to be added.

Activities of Daily Living (ADLs)

I use these *activities of daily living (ADLs),* listed on the next page, as a reminder of the different needs of my client. I also use them to interview an aide so that we're both clear about the elder's needs. This way, both the aide and I are in agreement as to what activities and tasks will need to be performed. I also ask the aide to write in a daily log or use this list as a check-off so that it's clear what was accomplished each day.

A senior might be able to accomplish some of these ADLs independently but need assistance with others. The senior's needs may change on a day-to-day basis, so the aide needs to clearly understand what's expected of him or her. You need to know that the aide has the training, education, and expertise to carry out these ADLs. Go over all details with the aide to ensure that he or she knows how to assist with every task listed on the next page. Note that they're listed alphabetically, not in order of importance, and that additional tasks may be needed for your elder.

Personal Care of the Elder

- Assistance to, in, and from the bathroom
- Assistance with bath: in bed or in a shower or tub
- Assistance with putting on or laying out clothes
- Assistance with toileting: bedpan, commode, and urinal
- Encouragement for the consumption of fluids per doctor's recommendation
- Feeding assistance, including both the use of adapted equipment and self-feeding
- Foot care assistance, including training in podiatry
- Hair care, including the application of beauty products, brushing, combing, and transporting to and from the beauty parlor/barber shop
- Incontinence care, including ensuring that supplies are always available
- Nail care (don't cut nails or cuticles), have this done by a professional
- Observation and reporting of changes in skin
- Oral (mouth) care/denture care
- Shaving assistance
- Skin care assistance and understanding what products should be used

Activities

- Assistance with ambulation
- Assistance with range of motion, but only with the advice of doctor or therapist
- Assistance with transfer in and out of a chair
- Attention to bed rails, which should be up at all times that elder is in bed
- Commitment to providing diversional activities, both in the home and in the community

Homemaking Assignments

- Cleaning of bathrooms, bedrooms, and kitchens
- Grocery shopping
- Laundry
- Light housekeeping
- Making and changing of bed
- Meal preparation

Hiring a Geriatric Care Manager

Many of you will read all or some of these 10 steps and decide you just can't manage the caregiving process alone. You don't have to. Do all you can in the time allotted. It's easy to become overwhelmed, but your elder's final days depend on your focused attention and energy. I realize this is much easier said than done.

If you're a long-distance caregiver, you may wish to hire a geriatric care manager to do a weekly follow-up. This consists of a visit with your elder and a phone call to the aide if one has been hired. Geriatric care managers can often help hire the right aide for your elder as well. I have a roster of aides who have worked with my clients over the years. They're very reliable and highly skilled. Agencies that train aides should also have well-qualified candidates available for you to interview.

Whether we choose it or not, caregiving is usually thrust upon us. And though we're not responsible for another person's happiness, we should always help a loved one in need. Determine what your resources are in terms of time, money, family, job, and travel. You have your own family, social life, and job responsibilities that can't be ignored. Figure out what you can do and what you can delegate to others. I discussed tapping into your family network as well as your elder's friends for help, but the best option can be to hire a geriatric care manager.

Each geriatric care manager has unique strengths and a special knowledge base, so someone you hire might have additional training, education, and experience. Below is a list of services that can be provided by most geriatric care managers.

- In-home assessment
- Institutional or hospital assessment
- Hospital visit in case of emergency
- Recommendation and implementation of adapted equipment
- Organizing of financial information
- Organizing of insurance information
- Making the home elder safe
- Arranging for meal service
- Hiring of cleaners, handy person, or assistants
- Streamlining of all medications
- Improving the elder's appearance
- Bringing entertainment into the home
- Serving as the communication hub for the family
- Understanding government entitlements and services that are available
- Arranging for travel to family events, or social gatherings
- Interviewing and hiring of aides and other home care personnel or medical specialists
- Monitoring the elder on an ongoing basis
- Recommending and arranging a higher level of care as required
- Crisis intervention
- Improving the elder's quality of life

Visit my website for further information on how and where to find a geriatric care manager in your area. Another authoritative resource is the National Association of Professional Geriatric Care Managers at www.caremanager.org. Be aware that fees will depend on your location and the level of experience and skills of the geriatric care manager in question.

As with all professionals that you are considering hiring, check out all references and letters of recommendations.

Step 10

Learn to Let Go

I wanted my soulmate's final days to take place in our home. We hired a daytime aide and then implemented hospice to make the transition as easy as possible. When my lover died, I knew we had both done our very best, but it was bittersweet. I eventually joined a support group to help with my grieving process.

—M.N., in Nevada

Every generation has a 100 percent mortality rate. Most people give me a weird look when I bring this up. But seriously, death is a certainty. Now is the time for you to think about how to deal with your loved one's death. Learn the values of your loved one and allow him or her to cope with this natural process. Allow yourself and others to express the complex needs associated with it, too.

Offering Solace
It's important that you learn how to offer solace and comfort while remaining comfortable in your own value system. Understand the various paths each individual takes to exit this life. Facing the unknown can be a structured experience, and being prepared can help everyone involved. Deal with the ethical issues in an open manner. Discover your elder's rich and valuable knowledge. Understand what your elder needs and wants, especially that he or she wants to be heard. Develop personal rituals for health, peace of mind, stress relief, and spiritual outlets.

When I was a young professional working in a nursing facility, a favorite resident of mine asked me for a glass of water. I gladly went off on my errand, and when I returned less than a minute later, he had passed away. That was when it first hit me how fragile and fleeting life is. You can be here one minute and gone the next, so you have to make the most of every moment.

When my younger sister was diagnosed with cancer, she was given one year to live and was told to get "her house in order." I was with her when she got the news. At first, she was devastated, but we soon decided to set goals—long-range goals. She had two young children and a wonderful husband, so she wanted to see her children attend high school, go to college, and get married. She wanted to know her grandchildren. At first, this seemed impossible, but we both persevered. It was so rewarding to be able to use my skills as a geriatric care manager with my sister. We went to workshops and tried alternative therapies. She lived another sixteen years—and she truly lived. Sometimes she was in remission, and other times she was in great distress. She traveled with her husband, and they retired after having fulfilled many of their goals and dreams. My sister eventually passed away a few weeks after holding her second grandchild.

Years ago, I was doing field work at a hospice center for college credit. I had been assigned to two boys (ages nine and ten), who had advanced cancer. One boy died during the second week I was there. But I was lucky enough to form a wonderful connection with the ten-year-old. We both liked to sing. During one weekend, his mother called me to say that her son was going to pass away in the next few days. She begged me to visit and sing with him, because he didn't like to sing with anyone else.

Of course, I dropped what I was doing and hurried to his bedside. I held him on my lap in a rocking chair, and we sang camp songs together. His mother was with us in the room. Suddenly, the boy seemed to become physically lighter in my arms. His mother called the doctor. At that moment, the boy opened his eyes and said, "Doctor Marion, don't be afraid of death. It's not so bad." With that, he passed on. That moment changed me forever.

I always tell my clients, "Don't be afraid of death. It's not so bad." Easy for me to say, right…but I firmly believe it! Preparations for the end of your loved one's life should begin today. My goal is to have your elder loved one pass on from this world with the utmost dignity, comfort, and respect. In this step I explain the dying process and give you practical skills for dealing with death and bereavement.

Fulfill Wishes

As I wrote earlier in this book, clear communication is the best way to involve your elder in end-of-life issues. Let him or her make decisions! Listen to your dying elder. Who was he or she for so many years? Learn about heartbreaks and heartthrobs. It's a golden opportunity for your elder to heal rifts and cement bonds forever.

Ask your elder how he or she wants to die. Death is a part of life—talk about it. Validate your elder's life. He or she needs someone to talk to. Your loved one might become quieter, sedentary, and lose interest in the outside world, and become more retrospective and introspective. Talk about highlights in life, such as a sweet sixteen, a prom, college, and children. You might discover fascinating things you never knew. One client told me all about her Rosie the Riveter days in the Brooklyn Navy yards. When I discussed this with her family, nobody ever knew this about her.

One way to ease the process is to prepare for the funeral with your loved one. You might find he or she is much more comfortable discussing the topic than everyone else is. If appropriate, pick out the clothing that will be worn at the funeral. Be sure you know what your elder wants done with his or her remains. Cultural differences are crucial. What rituals should be performed? If they're different from your traditions, learn about them and fulfill them.

One client of mine wanted to die with a three-iron next to him because that was the golf club he had used for his only hole-in-one. I arranged it for him, and his family loved it. I had another client who loved to go deep-sea fishing, and he asked that his ashes be scattered at sea. He said it would be the one time he didn't have to worry about getting seasick. Just be sure you're in compliance with the burial laws and regulations in your state.

Half of my clients have unresolved issues, and it truly hurts them. Preoccupation with the past is regret; preoccupation with the future is fantasy. What about living in the now? Living in hurt keeps us perpetual victims. In forgiveness, we may transcend hurt, loss, and grief. Try to help your elder work through these unresolved issues, and it'll make a big difference.

Your elder will probably want to be surrounded by people and things that give comfort. No substitutes, please. If Häagen Dazs vanilla bean ice cream is the request, don't come back with store-brand chocolate. Be sensitive to your elder's favorite smells, reading material, perfume, and so on. One man requested burial with his cherished photo of Marilyn Monroe. He said, "The Pharaohs were buried with their wives. I'll go down with my fantasy."

I once cared for a Greek patriarch who was dying a slow, difficult death from cancer. He wouldn't let go. After many weeks of struggle, I suggested that the eldest son tell his father that he was ready to take over the patriarch role for the family. He told his father in Greek, then in English, then in Greek again. The father smiled, wiped away a tear, and passed on five minutes later.

If possible, communicate with your elder about giving away family heirlooms and gifts. He or she will get much more from the experience if gifts are given to a favorite grandkid before passing on.

Have fun with a writing or communication exercise. I had another client who was a speakeasy hostess in the 1920s, and she had a lot of fun writing about it for her obituary. She wanted everyone to know that she had led an adventurous life! I suggest having your elder write out or verbally answer a few questions to get the conversation started.

- I feel deeply passionate about:
- I was put on this earth to:
- I've learned this from doing my work:
- I mean this to another person(s):
- I've learned this from my failures and mistakes:

- This moment or event was the turning point in my life:
- The angels in my life are:
- The miracles in my life are:
- I'd still like to accomplish:
- My mentors and role models have been:
- The books that have altered my thinking and/or changed my life:
- And this is my favorite! My single most valuable lesson in life is:

Preplanning

More and more individuals are looking to control the manner in which they die. The process can be more relaxed if all preplanning that can be done is done. Make sure you clearly understand what your elder wants, and then get it down on paper so that there isn't any confusion among family members and other loved ones. Not making this effort can destroy family dynamics at an extremely emotional, challenging time.

Face the business side of death by preparing final papers, the funeral arrangements, and final finances ahead of time. If you're able to preplan your elder's final days, draw from this list of details that can be executed:

- Get all legal papers in order.
- Prepare a will, a durable power of attorney, a health care proxy, and a living will.
- Discuss inheritance planning if it applies; then put a plan in place.
- Do an estate calculation, including federal and state estate taxes, final administration costs, and burial costs.
- Make sure the will and listed beneficiaries are current.
- Investigate lifetime gifts with a full understanding of your elder's cash flow projections.
- Discuss funeral details with your elder and have them taken care of upon the passing.

- Write your elder's obituary, or help him or her write it and include the most important facts and points of interest.

- Pick out funeral clothing.

- Inform the rest of the family what your elder's wishes are.

- Ask if your elder wants to be embalmed.

- Does he or she want an open or closed casket?

- Does he or she want to be cremated?

- Does he or she want organs donated?

- Arrange for transportation to the wake and the gravesite.

- Write the newspaper announcement when you write the obituary.

- Choose a newspaper to print the obituary.

- Determine how many people will attend the funeral and arrange for lodging for your out-of-town relatives.

- Find out how many people can be accommodated at the gravesite.

- Pick out the plot ahead of time if possible.

- Decide if lunch will be served after the service.

- Find out if your elder is eligible for military taps or honors if so desired.

- Ask if your elder is eligible to receive an armed forces flag.

- Buy a sign-in book and place it at the entrance of the funeral service.

- Find out if your loved one's remains require transportation to another state, and if so, arrange for transportation.

- Pay for the funeral arrangements in advance. It's often substantially less expensive, and you're far less likely to be taken advantage of if the arrangements have been paid before you're in crisis mode.

- Does your loved one want a private family viewing before the main event?
- Decide which flowers are appropriate.
- Determine if there's a favorite charity to which others may make a donation.
- Decide who will give the eulogy and if there should be multiple speakers.
- Decide if there will be a printed program.
- Decide if there will be music at the funeral, such as a flute or harp soloist.

Upon Death

As soon as possible after death, notify family members and friends, and then begin to oversee the funeral arrangements. You're also required by law to notify the Social Security department and all banks and other financial institutions. Other legal issues include informing the post office, closing or selling the home, taking care of any animals, changing the locks on the doors, and dividing assets according to the will.

You'll avoid headaches and certain delays if you get the death certificate immediately, rather than some time in the future. To be safe, you will need many original death certificates. You'll have to send them to all of your elder's financial institutions, as well as the Social Security office and other bureaucracies. There's usually a charge for each one.

The death certificate requires the following information:

- Full name
- Maiden name
- Social Security number
- Address
- Date of birth
- Date of death
- Military records
- Spouse's name
- Date of wedding
- Father and mother's name and maiden name

Grief

No amount of preplanning can eliminate grief, and it shouldn't. Even if you think you're prepared for a loved one's death, the pain is still immense. Grief is an important part of death. You have to allow yourself to feel it. It's healthy, and a powerful way to show love. Grief can be internalized through thoughts and feelings, but you need to allow yourself to externalize grief by expressing it in tears and words. We were given tear ducts to relieve the stress and pressure of our lives. That's what they are there for.

How do you comfort the people who are left behind? What are the right words? I suggest talking about an aspect of your elder's life that was most impressive. Focus on the positive. Emotions will come and go in waves. I strongly recommend that you allow yourself and others to express feelings, whatever they may be. But when death is imminent, focus on the details that you need to handle as the caregiver.

When my sister passed away, I didn't shed a tear because I was so focused on playing the caregiver role. Three months after she died, I pulled my car over to the side of the road and cried as deeply as I ever had before for thirty minutes! There I was, thinking: I'm a pro, I teach this; what's going on? I said all the right things to my family, but then the grief hit me.

So, I know what you're going through. Take care of yourself, too. Allow yourself to grieve, and then do something that makes you feel good, whatever that is. Go to a movie, shop, watch a ball game, or get a massage. You're in charge of allowing yourself to heal. You may heal slowly or quickly, but healing will come.

Beware of depression setting in. Many family members, especially the caregiver, can become depressed after the loss. Be aware if you find yourself overeating, not eating, drinking too much, chain-smoking, or any other such behavior. Grieving is hard work, so be sure you don't cut the process short. Get some sun. Share your grief with someone you can trust. Grieve in a way that feels right to you, not necessarily in a way that others have suggested. A crisis can be overwhelming if you look at all aspects of it at once. Take it one minute, one hour, one day at a time. If you think a professional could help you, arrange an appointment immediately with a therapist or grief counselor. Consider a grief support group. Many funeral homes offer them.

Considering Children

Although young children may not completely understand the event of death or the ceremony surrounding it, adults need to involve them in the experience and the funeral if this seems appropriate. This involvement helps establish a sense of comfort and the understanding that life goes on, even though someone they love has died.

Because the funeral is a significant event, children should have the same opportunity to attend as any other member of the family, as long as you and the other family members agree. They may be allowed to attend, but don't force them. Keep in mind that parents might need help explaining the purpose of the funeral, so it's an opportunity to help support and comfort each other, as well as a time to honor the life of the person who has died. Funerals provide a unique opportunity for the natural expression of grief and loss, and allow those attending to say "thank you" for the privilege of knowing and caring for your elder. This includes children when appropriate.

Don't assume every child in a certain age group understands death the same way or has the same feelings. Don't lie or tell half-truths to children. Don't wait to tell children what's happening. Keep them informed along the way. Encourage kids to ask questions about death, and be sure they know that you want to understand their concerns. Children's bodies react when they feel grief. Allow them to feel it. Don't feel you must have all of the answers for children about death and grieving. Finally, always keep information age-appropriate.

In Conclusion

Former Swedish Prime Minister Dag Hammarskjöld said, "Life only demands from you the strength you possess." I know that your caregiving challenge can be overwhelming. Take each day one minute, one hour at a time. In this caregiving process you can grow, better understand your values, change direction, face new challenges, help others, and learn to become a better listener. Many of us will learn to listen with our hearts and souls because we're in a different place due to our caregiving experience. If you think a professional could help you now, go ahead and arrange an appointment.

We're all in this life to share with and learn from each other. I've learned some new thought or insight from every one of my clients or their families, and it's my hope that the wisdom I've gained from them can help you during your caregiving experience. I'm so thankful to all of the clients and their family members who have let me into their lives, and I thank you for letting me share my experiences and knowledge with you. My hope is that you'll let me know about your caregiving journey.

Resources

I've compiled a list of many useful websites that I visit most often. Of course, there are others, and I encourage you to visit my website (www.doctormarion.com) for the most updated information.

AAA Foundation for Traffic Safety
www.aaafoundation.org/home

Academy of Nutrition and Dietetics
www.eatright.org

Access to Recreation
www.accesstr.com

Acupressure
www.verywellhealth.com/the-benefits-of-acupressure-88702

Administration on Aging
www.aoa.dhhs.gov

AirMed International
www.airmed.com

Alzheimer's Disease Education and Referral Center
www.alzheimers.org

American Academy of Dermatology
www.aad.org

American Academy of Facial Plastic and Reconstructive Surgery
www.aafprs.org

The American Academy of Ophthalmology
www.aao.org

American Academy of Otolaryngology
www.entnet.org

American Association for the Study of Liver Diseases (AASLD)
www.aasld.org

American Association of Homes and Services for the Aging
www.aahsa.org

American Association of Retired Persons (AARP)
www.aarp.org

American Bar Association (ABA)
www.abanet.org

American Board of Urology
www.abu.org

American Brain Tumor Association
www.hope.abta.org

American Council of the Blind
www.acb.org

American Dental Association
www.ada.org

American Diabetes Association
www.diabetes.org

American Gastroenterological Association
www.gastro.org

American Geriatrics Society
www.americangeriatrics.org

American Hearing Research Foundation
www.american-hearing.org

American Heart Association (AHA)
www.americanheart.org

American Institute of Certified Public Accountants
www.aicpa.org

American Liver Foundation
www.liverfoundation.org

American Medical Association
www.ama-assn.org

American Optometric Association
www.aoa.org

American Osteopathic Association
https://osteopathic.org

American Parkinson Disease Association
www.adaparkinson.org

Resources

American Psychiatric Association
www.psychiatry.org

American Red Cross
www.redcross.org

American Speech-Language-Hearing Association
www.asha.org

American Urogynecologic Society
www.augs.org

Brain Injury Association of America
www.biausa.org

Brookdale Center on Aging of Hunter College
www.brookdale.org

CBD Pain Free
www.buycbdpainfree.com
www.nutrasciencelabs.com
www.vitaleafnaturals.com

Certified Financial Planner Board of Standards
www.cfp-baord.org

Children of Aging Parents
www.caps4caregivers.org

Christopher and Dana Reeve Foundation
www.christopherreeve.org

Christopher Reeve Paralysis Foundation
www.apacure.com

Commission on Accreditation of Rehabilitation Facilities
www.carf.org

Community Transportation Association of America
www.ctaa.org

Council on Family Health
www.cfhinfo.org

Debby Bitticks
www.DebbyBitticks.com
Intergenerational Expert, Award Winning Author
Health and Caregiving Advocate
debby@debbybitticks.com
Co-Founder/Co-Creator, www.DigitalLifeCloud.com

Department of Veterans Affairs
www.va.gov

Disability Resources
www.disabilityresources.org

Disabled and Alone
www.disabledandalone.org

DrugHelp
www.drughelp.org

Easter Seals
www.easterseals.com

Elder Care Online
www.ec-inline.net

Elder Law Answers
www.elderlawanswers.org

Elder Web
www.elderweb.com

Enhanced Vision Systems
www.enhancedvision.com

Equal Employment Opportunity Commission
www.eeoc.gov

Family Caregiver Alliance
www.caregiver.org

Family Equality Council
www.familyequality.org

Federal Citizen Information Center
www.pueblo.gsa.gov

Federal Trade Commission
www.ftc.gov

Fifty Plus Magazine
www.50plusmag.com

Food and Drug Administration (FDA)
www.fda.gov

Funeral Consumers Alliance
www.funerals.org

Gerontological Society of America
www.eron.org

Grief Healing
www.griefhealing.com

Growth House
www.growthhouse.org

Guide Dog Foundation for the Blind
www.guidedog.org

Helping Hands Relocation
www.helpinghands-online.com

Hemlock Society
www.hemlock.org

Hospice Foundation of America
www.hospicefoundation.org

Hospice Helpline
www.nhpco.org

House of Representatives
www.house.gov

Insurance Information Institute
www.iii.org

Insurance Institute for Highway Safety
www.hwysafety.org

Interactive Aging Network
www.ianet.org

Joint Commission on Accreditation of Healthcare Organizations
www.jcaho.org

Lighthouse International
www.lighthouse.org

Little People of America
www.lpaonline.org

Managing Work and Family
www.mwfam.com

Mayo Clinic
www.mayoclinic.com

Meals on Wheels Association of America
www.mowaa.org

Medic Alert
www.medicaalert.org

Medicare
www.medicare.gov

Medicare Rights Center
www.medicarerights.org

Mr. Long-Term Care
www.mrltc.com

Multiple Sclerosis Association of America
www.msaa.com

National Academy of Elder Law Attorneys
www.naela.com

National Academy of Opticianry
www.nao.org

National Amputation Foundation
www.nationalamputation.org

National Aphasia Association
www.aphasia.org

National Association for Home Care and Hospice
www.nahc.org

National Association of Area Agencies on Aging
www.n4a.org

National Association of the Deaf
www.nad.org

National Caregiving Foundation
www.caregivingfoundation.org

National Center for Disability Services
www.ncds.org/index.asp

National Funeral Directors Association
www.nfda.org

National Guardianship Association
www.guardianship.org

National Headache Foundation
www.headaches.org

National Health Information Center
www.health.gov/nhic

National Highway Transportation Safety Administration
www.nhtsa.dot.gov

National Hospice and Palliative Care Organization
www.nho.org

National Institute of Arthritis and Musculoskeletal and Skin Diseases
www.niams.nih.gov

National Institute of Neurological Disorders
www.ninds.nih.gov

National Institute on Aging
www.nia.nih.gov

National Institute on Deafness and Other Communication Disorders
www.nidcd.nih.gov

National Mental Health Association
www.nmha.org

National Network of Estate Planning Attorneys
www.the.nnepa.com/public

National Osteoporosis Foundation
www.nof.org

National Registry of Rehabilitation Technology Suppliers
www.nrrts.org

National Rehabilitation Information Center
www.naric.com

National Respite Locator Service
www.respitelocator.org

National Safety Council
www.nsc.org

National Senior Citizens Law Center
www.nsclc.org

National Stroke Association
www.sstroke.org

National Vaccine Information Center
www.909shot.com

New Directions for People with Disabilities
www.newdirectionstravel.com

North American Securities Administrators Association
www.nasaa.org

Pension Benefit Guaranty Corporation
www.pbgc.gov

***Pro Se* Law Center**
pro-selaw.org

Reflexology
https://sciencebasedmedicine.org/iridology/
www.body-mindmassage.com/health-benefits-foot-massage-reflexology/
www.healthline.com/health/hand-reflexology

Reflexology Association of America
http://reflexology-usa.org

Road Scholars
www.roadscholar.org

Schizophrenia
www.schizophrenia.com

Schizophrenics Anonymous
www.nsfoundation.org/sa

Securities and Exchange Commission
www.sec.gov

Senior Law Home Page
www.seniorlaw.com

Seniors-site
www.seniors-site.com

Social Security Administration
www.ssa.gov

Society of Financial Service Professionals
www.financialpro.org

U.S. Consumer Products Safety Commission
www.cpsc.gov

U.S. Department of Housing and Urban Development
www.hud.gov

U.S. Department of Labor-Family and Medical Leave Act Advisor
www.dol.gov/elaws/fmla.htm

U.S. Senate
www.senate.gov

UI Medical, LLC
www.uimed.com
www.QuickChange.com

UrologyXY
www.urologyXY.org
www.urologyXY.com

Volunteers of America
www.voa.org

Well Spouse Foundation
www.wellspouse.org

White House
www.whitehouse.gov

Work and Family Connection
www.workfamily.com

Appendix A

Warning Signs

Because it's crucial to be proactive, carefully consider this alphabetical list of warning signs that could indicate a major change in your elder or prevent an oncoming crisis. Any one of these signs, or a combination thereof, is cause for alarm. These various warning signs can be caused by a reaction to a new medication, or they may just be the temporary symptom of nothing worse than a bad day. But they might indicate something serious, and it's definitely better to let your elder's primary care doctor know what's happening. He can refer your elder to a specialist for any additional diagnostic testing if required.

- Appearing wary about going from light to dark rooms and areas
- Bumping into walls, railings, or furniture
- Cuts and bruises appearing
- Depression
- Difficulty walking
- Falling
- Greater desire for sleep
- Hiding empty bottles of alcohol
- Hopelessness
- Incontinence
- Increased irritability
- Lack of ambition (even if the goals are modest)
- Lack of appetite
- Lack of interest in the holidays

- Lack of response to doorbell
- Leaving mail unopened
- Less fluid body movements
- Loss of focus
- Loss of interest in money
- Loss of self-confidence
- Loss of taste
- Mesmerized by a TV that is tuned to the same channel every day
- Mismatched shoes, socks, or clothing
- Mood swings and inconsistent behavior
- Not answering the phone or not calling family and friends
- Not caring for pets
- Not caring for plants
- Not changing out of pajamas
- Not showering
- Not hearing or comprehending verbal communication or instructions
- Not sending birthday or holiday cards
- Reduced spatial awareness
- Repeating what was just said, or asking you to repeat yourself
- Shunning social outings
- Sitting alone in an unlit room
- Skipping religious events
- Slurred speech
- Talking frequently about death
- Talking frequently about suicide
- Unkempt appearance
- Volume of TV or radio inappropriate: either too loud or too low
- Weight loss or gain

Elder Abuse

Be very aware that elder abuse happens all too often. Abuse can be emotional, physical, mental, financial, or a combination of any or all of the four. If you notice any strange bruises, ask your elder how they got there. If your elder seems fearful or there are other extreme changes in behavior, ask the tough questions. I've seen other family members, neighbors, and even hired help turn out to be guilty of elder abuse.

Hoarding

Hoarding is more than the accumulation of treasures and other items—it is when the material possessions run, interfere with, or endanger your elder's life. Many elderly accumulate items that serve no purpose, such as plastic shopping bags, plastic bottles, glasses, jars, magazines, and newspapers. These items can fall out of a closet or off of a shelf when you open a door. They may take up floor space.

But you cannot just come into your elder's environment and clean everything out. Often there are other factors involved in this sort of accumulation:

- When did the accumulation start?
- Why these particular items?
- Has your elder's judgment been compromised?
- Does he or she understand the impact this hoarding has on the environment, health, and neighbors?

Hoarding might need to be handled by a professional, as it's often a sign that something else is wrong with your loved one.

Appendix B

Alternative Therapies

I'm a staunch advocate of alternative therapies. Over the years, many of my clients have shown improvements in their cognitive and motor skills when I've implemented alternative therapies.

But I want to be very clear: I'm not explicitly recommending these therapies. Rather, I want you to know that there are other avenues to explore for your elder and yourself. Proceed with these programs only with the full knowledge and consent of your elder's primary care physician.

The alternative therapies are listed in alphabetical order.

Acupressure

Acupressure is an ancient Chinese healing method that treats body, emotions, mind, and spirit as one, not as separate parts. The human body has energy-carrying meridians from the fingertips to the brain to the organ associated with that meridian. The client lies on a massage table while the expert presses gently on various parts of the client's body. The average noninvasive session lasts for about one hour. Most clients require a number of sessions to achieve desired results.

Acupressure can help with the following:

- Stress and tension relief
- Mind and body relaxation
- Increased blood flow
- Toxic waste removal
- Relief of neck and shoulder aches
- Healing of injuries

- Increasing energy level
- Increasing feeling of well-being
- Decreasing labor pains

For more information, visit www.acupressure.com or www.nccaom.org.

Acupuncture

Acupuncture is the practice of inserting needles into the skin to stimulate specific anatomical points along the body's meridians for therapeutic purposes. Practitioners use heat, pressure, friction, suction, or impulses of electromagnetic energy to stimulate the points, along with the usual method of puncturing the skin with the fine needles. In traditional Chinese medicine, there are at least seven commonly used acupoints: transporting, five-element, yuan-source, xi-accumulating-cleft, mu-front-alarm, shu-back, and window to the sky. Each of the acupoints has specific positive effects on the different body currents and organs. For more information visit www.acupuncture.com or www.medicalacupuncture.org.

Alexander Technique

The Alexander technique is a way to understand the coordination of body and mind in order to free posture and remove unnecessary tension. It was developed by F. M. Alexander in the late 19th century, and is now taught in dance, acting, circus, and music schools. It has also been used to cure stuttering and improve ergonomics. Alexander was a Shakespearean orator who was always losing his voice when he tried to emote on stage. Observing himself in multiple mirrors, Alexander discovered that he was stiffening his body to recite his lines. He called his original principle "Direction." He discovered that a very slight head motion leads all physical body motion, acting as a steering wheel for the rest of the body, which must follow the head's lead. The Alexander technique can be practiced during any activity, and it can make body motion more efficient. For more details, visit www.alexandertechnique.com and www.alexandertech.org.

Applied Kinesiology

Applied kinesiology is a system that evaluates structural, chemical, and mental aspects of health by using manual muscle testing and other standard methods of diagnosis. A doctor using it finds an unbalanced muscle and tries to figure out why it's not functioning correctly. Treatments can involve joint manipulation or mobilization, various myofascial therapies, cranial techniques, meridian and acupuncture skills, clinical nutrition, dietary management, counseling skills, evaluating environmental irritants, and various reflex procedures. For more details, visit www.icak.com.

Aromatherapy

Aromatherapy is the art and science of using essential oils to relax, balance, and stimulate the body, mind, and spirit. Essential oils are the volatile aromatic essence produced by hundreds of aromatic plants through the process of photosynthesis. They can be used in a wide variety of ways for many different purposes, from curing athlete's foot to fostering enlightenment and all points between. You will find more information at www.accessnewage.com and at www.naha.org.

Art Therapy

Art therapy is premised on the belief that the creative process involved in making art is healing and life-enhancing. By creating and talking about art with a therapist, your elder can increase awareness of self, cope with stress and traumatic experiences, enhance cognitive abilities, and enjoy the life-affirming pleasures of artistic creativity. Visit www.arttherapy.org for details.

Cannabidiol (CBD)

As of 2019, cannabidiol (CBD) is everywhere—skin care, gummy bears, beverages and even pet treats. CBD is a natural substance that has become an accepted means of healing and relaxation. The most popular use of CBD currently is in the form of topical products such as creams and oils. One can provide direct relief to tired and inflamed muscles by simply applying a CBD topical to the sore area. CBD topicals usually provide relief within fifteen minutes by relaxing muscles and nerve cells, stimulating circulation, reduces pain and swelling.

Although hemp-derived CBD is legal in all fifty states, marijuana-derived CBD is not legal federally. Take note, both marijuana and hemp are members of the cannabis family making them similar in many ways. The government classifies hemp as any plant of the cannabis family that contains less than 0.3 percent THC (tetrahydrocannabinol). It classifies "marijuana" as any plant of the cannabis family that contains greater than 0.3 percent THC. Marijuana cannabis plants have a lower percentage of CBD than hemp plants. That's why most CBD products use CBD from hemp not marijuana. Because marijuana has higher concentration of THC, it's not an ideal choice for producing CBD products. Using marijuana plants would require extracting some of the THC to make CBD within the legal limits. Because there is no THC in CBD products that are marketed to the public, you do not need a prescription to purchase them.

There is not a federal guideline for legal age to purchase CBD products. Some local municipalities and states have set their own guidelines so you should check locally and see what your city and state have to say about this. There is nothing that states that a parent cannot give the products to children, however. In fact, there are products specifically marketed for children, as well as CBD for pets.

There is relatively little regulation on the CBD industry yet so "do you have to be eighteen to buy CBD?" is a question that can't be answered across the board. For now, it depends upon where you live and what your local laws are.

Chiropractic

Chiropractic practice is a science concerned with the relationship between the structure and function of the human body as it relates to your health. Chiropractic physicians don't prescribe drugs or perform surgery. Instead, they believe in the inherent power of the human body to heal itself. A chiropractor tries to facilitate the maintenance of a balanced, optimally functioning neuromusculoskeletal system. A chiropractic adjustment is a specific and precisely executed manual force directed to a joint in order to restore normal joint and nerve function. Websites with more information: www.chiro.org and www.amerchiro.org.

Color Therapy

Color therapy is based on the belief that physiological functions respond to specific colors. Some colors and their proven effects follow:

- *Black:* gives a sense of self-confidence, power, strength
- *Blue:* calms, lowers blood pressure, decreases respiration
- *Green:* soothes and relaxes; helps with depression, anxiety, nervousness
- *Orange:* energizes, stimulates appetite and digestive system
- *Pink:* suppresses appetite, relaxes muscles, relieves tension
- *Red:* stimulates brain waves, increases heart rate, excites sexual glands
- *Violet:* suppresses appetite, provides a peaceful environment, helps alleviate migraines
- *Yellow:* energizes, relieves depression, improves memory, stimulates appetite

Exposing the body to colored light is also believed to aid healing. Green light is believed to help heart problems and cancer, whereas blue is used to treat ulcer pain, inflammatory disorders, and back problems. Red is used to treat skin problems, bladder infections, and anemia, and orange works on allergies and constipation. Yellow light can alleviate muscle cramps, hypoglycemia, and gallstones. Visit www.colortherapyhealing.com.

Crystal Therapy

Crystal therapy was developed by the British inventor Harry Oldfield in the 1980s. It's based on the belief that the body has an energy field that can be influenced by the placement of crystals on specific body points to assist with physical, emotional, and spiritual balance and healing. It involves using an electromagnetic generator attached to conducting tubes filled with specific types of crystals. These tubes are applied to the body, and energy is transmitted through them. The crystals are selected for specific characteristics or wavelengths to treat a wide range of mental and physical conditions. More details are posted at www.healing.about.com/od/crystaltherapy.

Feldenkrais Method

The Feldenkrais method teaches students how to move their bodies more efficiently, improve coordination, expand range of motion, reduce stress on joints, and increase flexibility. Often sought out by those who have movement dysfunction and pain, the Feldenkrais method is also very popular with dancers, actors, musicians, and athletes. Russian-born physicist Moshe Feldenkrais (1904–1984) developed the method after he suffered a knee injury that was expected to prevent him from walking. A student of physics, psychology, and biology, Feldenkrais melded his diverse interests and knowledge to create his method, which he conceived while teaching himself to walk again without pain. The Feldenkrais method teaches you to listen to what your body is telling you. The method encourages awareness of one's skeleton, muscles, and joints, and also draws attention to negative patterns of posture and movement. The intent of the Feldenkrais practitioner is to enable students to refine their body awareness, so that each body part participates more fully in every action and no one body part is stressed more than any other. Visit www.Feldenkraisinstitute.org.

Guided Imagery

Guided imagery seeks to produce beneficial physical changes in the body via repeated visualization. A form of mind–body therapy, it has been advocated for a number of chronic conditions, including stress, anxiety, high blood pressure, and headaches, and for people undergoing conventional cancer therapy or surgery.

Described as a "focused daydream" by some practitioners, guided imagery is taught in small classes or one-on-one. You will be asked to wear comfortable clothing, and will either sit comfortably in a chair or lie on a table or a floor mat. Sessions usually begin with general relaxation exercises and then move on to a specific visualization described by the practitioner. You'll be asked to build a detailed image in your mind, using all five senses, and then repeat the exercise with a different image. If you have a specific medical complaint, the practitioner may ask you to picture your body free of the problem. Between sessions, you can use a book or audiotape to practice visualization on your own. For more information, visit www.guidedimageryinc.com.

Homeopathy

Homeopathic remedies are diluted solutions of assorted herbs, animal products, and chemicals. There are thousands of homeopathic remedies, and their alleged benefits cover just about every disease symptom imaginable. See websites: (abchomeopathy.com) and www.homeopathic.org.

Hypnosis

Hypnosis has been found to be effective for a variety of problems related to emotions, habits, and the body's involuntary responses. It won't cure underlying physical disorders such as cancer, heart disease, or infection, but it can relieve virtually all types of pain, no matter the source. It is also helpful in guarding against anxiety, tension, depression, phobias, and compulsions, and it can sometimes help break an addiction to smoking, alcohol, or drugs.

Modern hypnotherapy relies on induction of a "trance-like" state to reach the unconscious level of the mind, over which people usually have no control. After the unconscious is open to suggestion, you and your therapist can more easily change the way you perceive problems, and promote new ways of responding to them.

Hypnosis doesn't work for everyone. For those who are susceptible, however, it has successfully alleviated an amazing range of conditions, including asthma, allergies, stroke, multiple sclerosis, Parkinson's disease, cerebral palsy, and irritable bowel syndrome. It can control nausea and vomiting from cancer medications, reduce bleeding during surgery, steady the heartbeat, and bring down blood pressure. It has helped some people lose weight, control severe morning sickness, and get relief from muscle spasms and even paralysis. Visit www.hypnosis.com.

Iridology (Iris Reading)

Iridology is the study of the iris to diagnose disease. It's based on the assumption that every organ in the human body has a corresponding location within the iris, and that determining whether an organ is healthy or diseased can be done by examining the iris rather than the organ itself.

Ignatz von Péczely, a 19th-century Hungarian physician, invented iridology. He got the idea when he saw a dark streak in the eyes of a man he was treating for a broken leg, and it reminded him of a similar dark streak in the eyes of an owl who had broken its leg years earlier. Von Péczely went on to document similarities in eye markings and illnesses in his patients; then others completed the mapping of the eye. Visit www.skepdic.com/iridol.html.

Kirlian Photography

In 1939 Semyon Kirlian discovered that if an object on a photographic plate is subjected to a high-voltage electric field, an image is created on the plate. The image looks like a colored halo or a coronal discharge. This image is said to be a physical manifestation of the spiritual aura or "life force" that, it is said, surrounds each living thing. Allegedly, this special method of "photographing" objects is a gateway to the paranormal world of auras. Website: www.kirlian.com.

Magnetic Field Therapy

This therapy is usually prescribed to relieve muscle and joint pain, headaches, carpal tunnel syndrome, muscle strains, hip and joint pain, arthritis, fibromyalgia, osteoarthritis, persistent rotator cuff tendonitis, chronic pelvic pain, and sprains of the spine, neck, or limbs. Magnetic fields are sometimes used to speed the healing of bone fractures, and to relieve stress, combat infections, and prevent seizures. For pain management, small magnetic discs are usually taped to the body over the areas that radiate the pain. Magnets used for this type of therapy typically generate a field measured at ten times the strength of a typical refrigerator magnet. Visit www.painrelief.org.

Massage Therapy

Massage cannot cure serious medical disorders, but it can provide relief from the symptoms of anxiety, tension, depression, insomnia, and stress, as well as back pain, headache, and muscle pain. It's also frequently recommended for the treatment of minor sports injuries and repetitive stress injuries, and for increasing physical conditioning. Visit www.massagetherapy.com and www.amtamassage.org.

Meditation

Meditation is a deliberate suspension of the stream of consciousness that usually occupies the mind. Its primary goal is to induce mental tranquility and physical relaxation. Meditation is a proven antidote for stress, tension, anxiety, and panic. Meditation is also a scientifically verified way of reducing high blood pressure and relieving chronic pain. Many people find it helpful for headaches and respiratory problems such as emphysema and asthma.

At the outset, whatever the form of meditation, you need to wear comfortable clothes and assume a sitting position where the spine is vertical. Slow, rhythmic breathing is a necessity in all forms of meditation, although each approach has a different way of achieving this. As you sit quietly and breathe rhythmically, you must focus on something—it may be your own breathing, or an image such as a religious symbol, a flower, or candle, or a word or phrase repeated rhythmically. Visit www.learingmeditation.com.

Music Therapy

Music therapy uses music to address the physical, emotional, cognitive, and social needs of individuals of all ages. It can improve the quality of life of children and adults with disabilities or illnesses. Music therapy can promote wellness, manage stress, alleviate pain, help to express one's feelings, enhance memory, improve communication, and promote physical rehabilitation. Websites: www.musictherapyworld.de and www.musictherapy.org.

Neuro-Linguistic Programming

Neuro-linguistic programming (NLP) therapists try to detect any ingrained, unconscious attitudes that may be interfering with your body's natural healing abilities. Have you unconsciously despaired over your recovery? If so, you may reveal your feelings in the way you describe your illness. NLP therapists also look for clues in your facial expressions and body language, and even in the amount of moisture on your lips or eyes, or subtle changes in your skin color.

The goal of this form of therapy is to reprogram your automatic mental and physical responses, replacing debilitating patterns with reactions that promise to combat your illness. By teaching you to substitute more positive thoughts and images for the previously negative thinking and imagery, neuro-linguistic practitioners hope to remove the psychological roadblocks that obstruct the body's natural healing mechanisms. Visit www.nlpinfo.com.

Occupational Therapy

Occupational therapists work with individuals who have conditions that are mentally, physically, developmentally, or emotionally disabling. They help them develop, recover, or improve daily living and work skills to lead independent, productive, and satisfying lives. Visit www.occupationaltherapist.com and www. aota.org.

Osteopathy

Born over a century ago from the belief that displaced bones, nerves, and muscles are at the root of most ailments, osteopathy has long since been in the medical mainstream. Although originally used to treat all forms of disease, osteopathic manipulation is now considered useful primarily for musculoskeletal disorders such as back and neck pain, joint pain, sciatica, sports injuries, repetitive stress injuries, and some types of headache. Visit www.osteopathy.html.

Pets and Robotic Comfort Companions

Pets can be wonderful companions for our aging loved ones. They provide comfort and love and give the elderly person a purpose when living alone. However, caring for a pet can be a lot of work especially for an aging loved one.

Innovations in robotic companion pets are growing all the time. These robotic cats, dogs etc provide the same level of comfort for an aging loved one without the work, expense, allergies and possible hazards.

For senior citizens in need of companionship who aren't able to care for a real animal, these robotic cats and dogs look, feel, and act pretty much like the real thing. Thanks to built-in sensors, they purr and nuzzle when touched; they also meow, sleep, and roll over for belly rubs. Just like any beloved pet, these pets keep the secrets you share with them forever. Pet therapy is often suggested in supporting a person with a variety of disorders. A robotic comfort companion can open up conversations among elderly people and other friends and relatives and can provide a shared source of entertainment for grandchildren. Before purchasing a pet for your elderly loved one, consider a robotic companion pet. Information for companion pets can be found in the Resources section.

Psychiatrists

These doctors work with people with mental, emotional, or addictive disorders. They can diagnose and treat depression, schizophrenia, substance abuse, anxiety disorders, and sexual and gender identity issues. Some psychiatrists focus on children, adolescents, or the elderly.

Physical Therapy

Physical therapists help restore function, improve mobility, relieve pain, and prevent or limit permanent physical disabilities. Their patients include accident victims and individuals with disabling conditions such as low-back pain, arthritis, heart disease, fractures, head injuries, and cerebral palsy. They also restore, maintain, and promote overall fitness and health.

Therapists examine a patient's medical history and then test and measure the patient's strength, range of motion, balance and coordination, posture, muscle performance, respiration, and motor function. They determine the patient's ability to be independent and to reintegrate into the community or workplace after injury or illness. Physical therapists also develop treatment plans with a full treatment strategy, purpose, and anticipated outcome. Visit www.apta.org.

Pilates

The Pilates method is designed to lengthen and strengthen muscles while improving balance, posture, coordination, strength, flexibility, and balance. It's an effective way to rehabilitate the body after injuries and chronic pain. Visit www.pilatesmethodalliance.org.

Qigong

The exercises of this Chinese discipline can reduce stress and anxiety, and improve overall physical fitness, balance, and flexibility. By alleviating tension, they may also combat insomnia and relieve certain types of headache. In traditional Chinese medicine, however, Qigong (pronounced "chee-gong") is credited with much more. Proponents claim it has cured cancer, heart disease, AIDS, arthritis, and asthma. They also recommend it for migraines, hemorrhoids, constipation, diabetes, high blood pressure, menstrual problems, prostate trouble, impotence, and pain. Some say it even corrects nearsightedness and farsightedness.

Wear loose, comfortable clothing and flexible shoes (no sneakers) when you exercise with this method. Do not eat or drink anything, especially alcoholic beverages, within ninety minutes of your Qigong sessions. If you find you cannot follow all three aspects of an exercise—visualizing, moving, and breathing—at the same time, concentrate first on visualization. Visit www.qi.org.

Reality Orientation

Over time, individuals with Alzheimer's disease may withdraw from contact with others and the environment as they become increasingly disoriented. This withdrawal results in a lack of sensory stimulation. To prevent understimulation, a therapy called reality orientation was developed. This practice is based on the belief that continually and repeatedly stating or showing certain reminders to people with mild to moderate memory loss will result in increased interaction with others and improve their orientation.

This in turn can improve self-esteem and reduce problem behaviors. In reality orientation, people with Alzheimer's disease are surrounded by familiar objects that can be used to stimulate

Hand Reflexology Chart

right palm   left palm

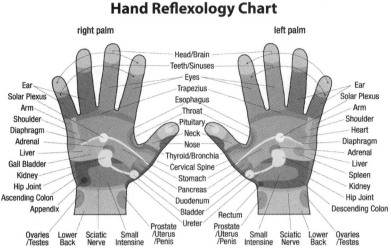

right palm				center labels				left palm

Head/Brain
Teeth/Sinuses
Eyes
Ear
Solar Plexus
Arm
Shoulder
Diaphragm
Adrenal
Liver
Gall Bladder
Kidney
Hip Joint
Ascending Colon
Appendix

Trapezius
Esophagus
Throat
Pituitary
Neck
Nose
Thyroid/Bronchia
Cervical Spine
Stomach
Pancreas
Duodenum
Bladder
Ureter
Prostate
/Uterus
/Penis

Ear
Solar Plexus
Arm
Shoulder
Heart
Diaphragm
Adrenal
Liver
Spleen
Kidney
Hip Joint
Descending Colon

Rectum
Prostate
/Uterus
/Penis

Ovaries /Testes | Lower Back | Sciatic Nerve | Small Intensine | | | Small Intensine | Sciatic Nerve | Lower Back | Ovaries /Testes

their memory. Other materials, such as family scrapbooks, flash cards, a Scrabble game, a globe, large-piece jigsaw puzzles, and illustrated large-print dictionaries, are also helpful. Visit www.zarcrom.com/users/alzheimers/4-14.htm.

Recreational Therapy

Recreational therapists provide treatment services and recreation activities to individuals with disabilities or illnesses. Using a variety of techniques, including arts and crafts, animals, sports, games, dance and movement, drama, music, and community outings, therapists treat and maintain the physical, mental, and emotional well-being of their clients. Therapists help individuals reduce depression, stress, and anxiety; recover basic motor functioning and reasoning abilities; build confidence; and socialize effectively so that they can enjoy greater independence. In health care settings in hospitals and rehabilitation centers, recreational therapists treat and rehabilitate individuals with specific health conditions, usually in conjunction or collaboration with physicians, nurses, psychologists, social workers, and physical and occupational therapists.

In long-term and residential care facilities, recreational therapists use leisure activities to improve and maintain their clients' general health and well-being. Visit www.bls.gov/oco/ocos082.htm and www.atra-tr.org.

Reflexology

Reflexologists use their hands to apply pressure to specific points of your foot. Typically, you sit with your legs raised or lie back on a treatment table. After gently massaging your foot, the

Foot Reflexology Chart

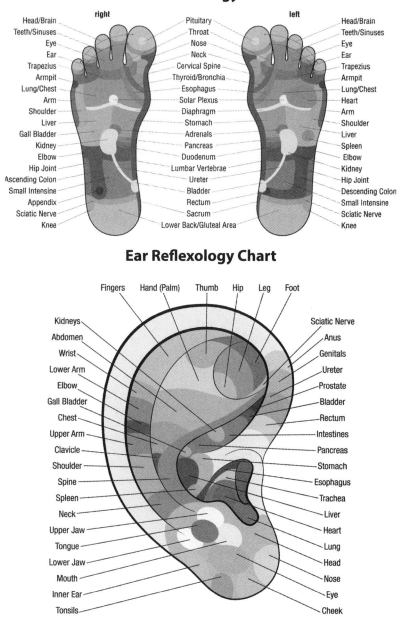

Ear Reflexology Chart

reflexologist will apply pressure to the reflex points thought to correspond to your health problems. If you have foot problems, such as severe calluses or corns, the therapist may refer you to a podiatrist for treatment. Although most reflexologists work only with the feet, they don't treat foot disorders.

Many reflexologists say that manipulation of the feet reduces the amount of lactic acid in the tissues by releasing tiny calcium crystals that accumulate in the nerve endings and hold back the free flow of energy to corresponding organs. Others speculate that pressure on the reflex points may trigger the release of endorphins (chemicals in the brain that naturally block pain). Visit www.reflexology-usa.org.

Pressure Points on the Body, Hands, and Feet

Reflexology is the application of pressure to areas on the feet, hands, and ears. Reflexology is generally relaxing and can be an effective way to alleviate stress.

Reflexologists use foot charts to guide them as they apply pressure to specific areas. Practitioners of reflexology include chiropractors, physical therapists, and massage therapists, among others.

Numerous studies funded by the National Cancer Institute and the National Institutes of Health indicate that reflexology may reduce pain and psychological symptoms, such as anxiety and depression, and enhance relaxation and sleep. Studies also show that reflexology may have benefits in palliative care of people with cancer.

Reflexology is generally considered safe, although very vigorous pressure may cause discomfort for some people. Reflexology is a quick and easy way to bring comfort to yourself or the person you are caring for.

Hand Reflexology

Hand reflexology is a massage technique that puts pressure on various reflex points around your hands. The belief is that these points correlate to different body parts and that massaging the points can help to relieve symptoms in other areas of the body. These include: anxiety, constipation, and headaches:

Foot Reflexology

Reflexology is an ancient healing practice based on the principle that there are reflex points on the feet that correspond to the body's different organs and glands. The human foot has almost 15,000 nerve endings.

In reflexology pressure is applied to these reflexes on the feet, which promotes good health. Here are some health benefits of foot massage and reflexology: Improves blood circulation; fights depression; helps in relaxation; promotes better sleep; and relieves body pains.

Ear Acupressure

Ear acupressure (also called *auriculotherapy* or simply *ear treatments*) can help you reduce symptoms of discomfort and stay healthy. Using ear treatment methods, you can address everything from stress reduction and boosting immunity to soothing your digestion, easing joint and muscle pains, and more.

Everyone at every stage of life is sensitive to the light soothing touch of the ears. A few years ago, while on a long flight a young couple were struggling with an infant whose shrill crying was disrupting everyone on the red-eye. I was walking the aisle and asked the parents if I may give them a break and walk with the baby in my arms as I am a parent and grandmother as well. While walking with the infant I gently rubbed her ears. Within ten minutes the infant was asleep in my arms.

Bowel Movements: Shape and Frequency

Doctors in gastroenterology and hepatology specialize in preventing, diagnosing, and treating digestive tract and liver disorders. These mainly include conditions involving the pancreas, liver, gallbladder, esophagus, stomach, small intestine, and colon.

Bowel habits can vary from person to person. This includes how often you have a bowel movement, your control over when you have a bowel movement, and the bowel movement's consistency and color. Alterations in any aspect of these habits over the course of a day represent a change in bowel habits.

Although some bowel movement changes can represent temporary infections, others may indicate greater cause for concern. Knowing when to seek medical help can prevent an emergency condition from worsening.

Colon and Rectal Surgeons

You would see these doctors for problems with your small intestine, colon, and bottom. They can treat colon cancer, hemorrhoids, and inflammatory bowel disease. They also can do a colonoscopy and other tests for colon cancer.

Feces

The Heaton stool chart is designed to help doctors measure the time it takes for food to pass through your body and leave as waste. The shape and form of your poop may also point your doctor toward a diagnosis of some digestive problems.

Heaton Stool Chart

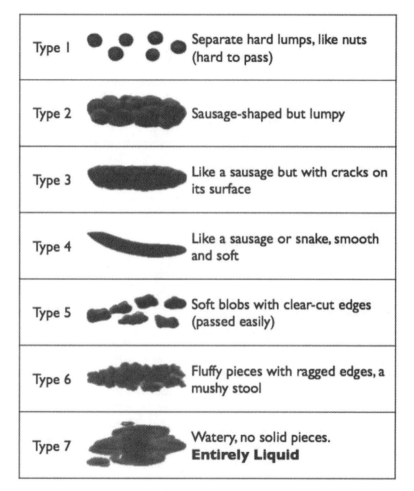

Type 1	Separate hard lumps, like nuts (hard to pass)
Type 2	Sausage-shaped but lumpy
Type 3	Like a sausage but with cracks on its surface
Type 4	Like a sausage or snake, smooth and soft
Type 5	Soft blobs with clear-cut edges (passed easily)
Type 6	Fluffy pieces with ragged edges, a mushy stool
Type 7	Watery, no solid pieces. **Entirely Liquid**

Ken Heaton, M.D., from the University of Bristol, developed the chart in 1997 with the help of sixty-six volunteers. They changed their diets, swallowed special marker pellets, and kept a diary about their bowel movements: weight, shape, and how often they went.

Brown poop—the normal color of poop is brown and is in the shape of a perfectly shaped banana with no residue

Black poop—foods such as black licorice and many blueberries can turn your poop black. Long-term constipation can also turn poop black.

Urine Color Chart

Dark yellow urine is often indicative of dehydration.

Yellowing or **light orange** urine may be caused by removal of of excess B vitamins from the bloodstream.

Pinkish urine can result from the consumption of beets.

Orange urine can be caused by certain medications such as rifampin and phenazopyridine.

Greenish urine can result from the consumption of asparagus.

Red or bloody urine is termed *hematuria,* a symptom of a wide variety of medical conditions.

Reddish or **brown** urine may be caused by porphyria.

Dark orange to **brown** urine can be a symptom of jaundice, rhabdomyolsis, or Gilbert's syndrome.

Blue urine can be caused by the ingestion of methylene blue.

Black or **dark-colored** urine is referred to as melanuria and may be caused by a melanoma.

Purple urine may be due to purple urine bag syndrome.

If poop is black for too long (three or more days) it can be due to intestinal issues and one should consult a doctor.

Green poop—too much fiber and too many greens can turn your poop green. If this condition persists it could be due to gallbladder issues from excess bile. Consult a doctor if this condition persists.

Pale yellow poop—clay textured pale yellow poop could be a result of medications taken, or it may be a result of gallbladder or pancreatic conditions. Consult your doctor if this persists beyond three to four days.

Yellow poop—if yellow poop has an increased odor it could be the result of food stagnation that can cause inflammation or gallbladder issues. Please consult your doctor should you have concerns.

Red poop—when one eats foods like beets or red Jell-O or other foods that have red food color it can effect poop. If this is not a dietary issue it could be blood in the poop. Please consult your doctor should you have concerns.

A balanced diet of veggies, starch, and protein and enough water is important to your diet. Consult your doctor should you have any concerns regarding persistent problems.

Urologists

These are surgeons who care for men and women with problems in the urinary tract, like a leaky bladder, and they also do prostate exams.

Normal urine is clear and has a straw-yellow color. While the odor of urine can vary somewhat, in most cases, it does not have a strong smell. With dehydration, the urine is more concentrated and may have a stronger ammonia scent than normal. Consumption of certain foods, such as asparagus (which can impart a characteristic odor to urine), and taking some medications may be causes for changes in the odor of urine. The presence of bacteria in the urine, such as with a *urinary tract infection (UTI),* can affect the appearance and smell of urine. When there is an infection in the urinary tract, the urine may take on a foul-smelling odor as well as appear cloudy or bloody. A burning sensation during urination may be a symptom of a UTI. The urine may also have an abnormally sweet odor in uncontrolled diabetes, and some rare genetic conditions can also cause the urine to have an abnormal or strange odor.

Nail Reading

Your nails can reveal clues to your overall health. A touch of white here, a rosy tinge there, or some rippling or bumps may be a sign of disease in the body. Problems in the liver, lungs, and heart can show up in your nails.

Tongue

Both the top of the tongue and underneath the tongue are indicators of the state of your health.

Relaxation Therapy

Relaxation therapies differ in philosophy and method. The goal is to use the power of the mind and body to achieve a sense of relaxation. Relaxation therapies often focus on repeating a sound, word, or prayer. They also may focus on a body sensation. Passive attitudes help ward off intruding thoughts. Relaxation therapies can lower the metabolism and make a person feel at peace, and can help treat chronic pain and insomnia. Visit www.healthyplace.com.

Rolfing

Rolfing improves general well-being by relieving stress, improving mobility, and boosting energy. The deep massage techniques employed in Rolfing seek to loosen and relax the fascia—the membranes that surround the muscles. To break up knots in the fascia and "reset" the muscles, Rolfers apply slow, sliding pressure with their knuckles, thumbs, fingers, elbows, and knees. The treatments are not mild and relaxing—indeed, they can cause a degree of pain. Practitioners view this temporary discomfort as a sign that the treatment is achieving the changes necessary to bring the body back into proper alignment.

Before beginning the treatments, your therapist will take a full medical and personal history, and evaluate your posture and body structure for signs of tension and misalignment. The treatments themselves are performed while you lie or sit on a massage table or floor mat. During each session, the Rolfer will concentrate on a different set of muscles, starting with those nearest the surface and moving on to those deep within the body. Visit www.crystalinks.com/rolfing.html and www.rolf.org.

Shiatsu

Shiatsu practitioners believe that vital energy (Ki in Japanese) flows throughout the body in a series of meridians. Shiatsu practitioners consider your state of health and the symptoms you have experienced, and will use a variety of techniques to improve your energy flow. These may include gentle holding; pressing with palms, thumbs, fingers, elbows, knees, and feet on the meridians; and, when appropriate, more dynamic rotations and stretches. As the quality of Ki changes, the symptoms associated with a lack of energy flow will gradually improve. Visit www.shiatsu.org.

Spiritual Healing

Spirituality involves the recognition and acceptance of a God beyond our own intelligence with whom we can have a relationship. This God can provide an experience of inspiration, joy, security, peace of mind, and guidance that goes beyond what is possible in the absence of the conviction that God exists. Spiritual healing works on the body, mind, and spirit, which are seen as one unit that must harmonize for good health. The healing energy from this source is available to all. Any problem, be it a broken leg or depression, needs the power of healing to restore the balance of the whole person. Sickness often starts in the mind, or at the deeper level of the spirit, and it's often here where healing begins. Visit www.1stholistic.com/Prayer/hol_spiritual_healing.htm.

Tai Chi

This slow, graceful Chinese exercise program pays dividends in increased strength and muscle tone, enhanced range of motion and flexibility, and improved balance and coordination. Many who practice tai chi find that it also offers a variety of "quality of life" benefits such as improved concentration, an increased sense of well-being, decreased stress, more energy, improved posture, and better circulation. Derived from the martial arts, this low-intensity, low-impact form of exercise is especially well suited to those recovering from an injury. And because it's a weight-bearing exercise, it can also be helpful in preventing osteoporosis.

Tai chi exercises encompass a set of "forms." With names like "Grasping the Bird's Tail" and "Wave Hands Like Clouds," each form consists of a series of positions strung together into one continuous movement, including a set beginning and end. A single form may include up to 100 positions and may take as long as twenty minutes to complete. The forms can be performed anywhere at any time, but for maximum health benefits, tai chi experts recommend setting aside the same time every day. In China, tai chi is often performed in large groups as an early morning exercise. Visit www.chebucto.ns.ca/Philosophy/Taichi.

Therapeutic Touch

Therapeutic touch proponents say the practice heals wounds, relieves tension headaches, and reduces stress. Similar to massage, it's usually employed as a supplement to, rather than a replacement for, standard medical therapies. It's sometimes used to relieve discomfort between scheduled doses of pain medication for hospitalized patients, and is also employed by hospice nurses to relieve pain in terminally ill patients, and to help families accept the death of a loved one. Visit www.therapeutictouch.com and www.therapeutictouch.org.

Trager Integration

This light, gentle form of massage seeks to release deeply ingrained tensions to promote a sense of relaxation and freedom. It can be especially helpful for people with chronic neuromuscular pain, including back problems and sciatica, and it has also been advocated for stress-related conditions, high blood pressure, strokes, migraines, and asthma. Proponents say that it can benefit patients with polio, multiple sclerosis, and muscular dystrophy.

Also known as *Tragerwork* or the *Trager approach,* this form of therapy has two components: bodywork conducted by the therapist, and a set of movement exercises to be pursued between treatments. Trager therapists believe that the deeply relaxed feelings the technique induces can resonate throughout the nervous system, ultimately benefiting tissues and organs deep within the body. Visit www.wellspring.co.nz/practices/Tragerwork/tragerwork.htm.

Yoga

Yoga offers a variety of proven health benefits. It increases the efficiency of the heart and slows the respiratory rate, improves fitness, lowers blood pressure, promotes relaxation, reduces stress, and allays anxiety. It also serves to improve coordination, posture, flexibility, range of motion, concentration, sleep, and digestion. It can be used as supplementary therapy for conditions as diverse as cancer, diabetes, arthritis, asthma, migraines, and AIDS, and helps to combat addictions such as smoking.

A typical session includes three disciplines: breathing exercises, body postures, and meditation. Many proponents feel morning is the best time to practice yoga, but classes are offered throughout the day and evening. It's advisable to avoid eating for one hour before class. Each session usually begins with a set of gentle warm-up exercises. The teacher will then ask you to focus on your breathing, and may take you through several breathing exercises. Then it's on to a series of poses that typically must be held for periods of a few seconds to several minutes. Unlike the routine in calisthenics or weight training, you will not be asked to repeat postures more than three times, and some will be done only once.

Some of the postures, such as shoulder rolls or neck stretches, will probably be familiar to you, while others may seem extremely complicated and strangely contorted. Despite the difficulty of such postures, however, contortion for its own sake is never the point. The goal is to mildly stretch all of the muscle groups in the body, while gently squeezing the internal organs. To balance the muscle groups, the postures follow a specific order. As you assume the various postures, you'll be asked to move gently, without jerking or bouncing. Breathing techniques remain important, and you'll need to focus on exhaling during certain movements and inhaling during others.

Likewise, as you hold certain postures, you may be instructed to inhale through one nostril and exhale through the other. You'll be allowed to rest after every three or four postures, and at the conclusion of the exercises, there's usually a period of rest or meditation. You should remain comfortable throughout the session, and should leave with both body and mind relaxed. Visit www.yogabasics.com and www.yogadirectory.com.

Appendix C

Understanding Various Body Parts

This section of the book outlines different medical specialists that one may need to call upon when caring for an elderly loved one or oneself.

Simplified, clarified, and organized, this section has been designed to make it easy for anyone looking for clarification on what doctor and specialist one may need.

Skin/Nails/Hair

The maintenance of skin integrity is of primary of importance. The skin, nails, and hair are often easily observable indicators of overall health. Neglecting skin issues can cause larger health issues in the long run.

Weight issues (*see* Appendix A) can affect skin care and skin integrity. Anyone who is overweight to being bariatric often finds themselves incontinent at an earlier age; research indicates that the age of being incontinent is becoming younger and younger as our society becomes heavier. As a caregiver, this is an issue that requires attention and needs to be to addressed. The amount of food we ingest is in our control. We must take care in what we feed ourselves and the ones for whom we are caring.

Dermatologists

Dermatologists specialize in your skin, hair, and nails. They are rained to treat moles, scars, acne, and skin allergies. A dermatologist can also provide support for cosmetic issues.

It is important to know that you are visiting a licensed or certified dermatologist.

Incontinence-Associated Dermatitis (IAD) Skin Care

Many people who have incontinence will experience incontinence-associated dermatitis (IAD) at one point or another. This is especially common in older adults.

Incontinence refers to your body's inability to control the release of urine or stool. IAD occurs when the protective barrier created by your skin is damaged.

Exposure to the bacteria in urine or stool can result in painful symptoms, such as burning and itching. The condition primarily affects the area around your genitals, thighs, and abdomen.

You should have your doctor review any area you suspect is affected by the condition. Your doctor will help you determine how to best manage and treat your incontinence and IAD. In most cases, IAD is temporary and will clear up with treatment.

IAD may also be referred to as *perineal dermatitis, irritant dermatitis, moisture lesions,* or even *diaper rash,* though these are all different conditions.

Managing IAD goes along with managing incontinence. You should see your doctor to discuss management plans for both conditions. Attention to skin cleanliness is important to the skin area.

If you do have IAD, treating the condition is essential to controlling its severity. If left untreated, IAD can lead to additional complications. Using proper prevention techniques will lessen your chances of experiencing IAD flare-ups in the future.

Anyone who has ever diapered a child knows that one must attend to a dirty diaper quickly to avoid diaper rash. When urine and feces mingle on the skin, the skin breaks down faster. When one has the opportunity to localize the urine outflow so that it does not pool under the buttocks or leak down the legs/thighs it helps to ameliorate the exacerbation of these two chemical sources meeting.*

*The Tip Of The Spear: this particular article written by Dr. Marion Somers and Marc Harris discusses the subject of the urine and feces meeting and causing skin disruption.

Incontinence

Do not ignore the early signs of incontinence. This is a situation that when addressed early on can be treated. Understanding how urine and/or feces on the skin effect the skin when not cleaned properly is important. There are many products on the market for adults with incontinence issues. For a woman, any drug store or surgical/medical supply stores will have a variety of female incontinent products. They come in different sizes, absorption, styles, and functionalities to meet different needs.

Medical Specialties by Body Regions

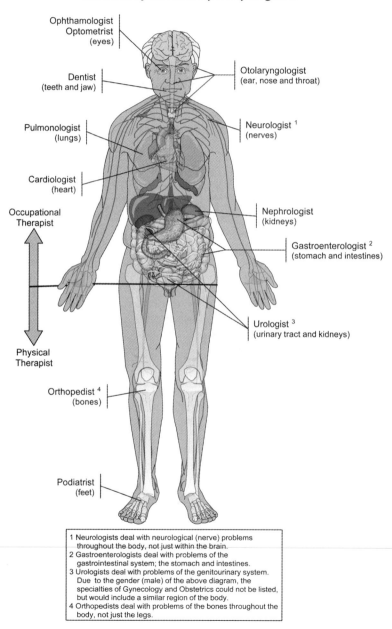

Ophthamologist
Optometrist
(eyes)

Otolaryngologist
(ear, nose and throat)

Dentist
(teeth and jaw)

Pulmonologist
(lungs)

Neurologist [1]
(nerves)

Cardiologist
(heart)

Occupational
Therapist

Nephrologist
(kidneys)

Gastroenterologist [2]
(stomach and intestines)

Physical
Therapist

Urologist [3]
(urinary tract and kidneys)

Orthopedist [4]
(bones)

Podiatrist
(feet)

1 Neurologists deal with neurological (nerve) problems
  throughout the body, not just within the brain.
2 Gastroenterologists deal with problems of the
  gastrointestinal system; the stomach and intestines.
3 Urologists deal with problems of the genitourinary system.
  Due to the gender (male) of the above diagram, the
  specialties of Gynecology and Obstetrics could not be listed,
  but would include a similar region of the body.
4 Orthopedists deal with problems of the bones throughout the
  body, not just the legs.

Men might have different needs regarding incontinence than women due to their body. There are many new products that can make caring for an incontinent man easier for the caregiver. These include male briefs that are absorbent and the QuickChange Wrap that isolates the urine, keeping it from migrating to the buttocks, thighs, and abdomen.

When being the caregiver to someone with incontinence it is important to be hyper vigilant about skin integrity. This requires regularly checking the incontinence briefs and using barrier creams. Being a caregiver to a non-ambulatory person is very different from caring for someone who is more mobile and is able to walk. Being a caregiver to a person who is non-ambulatory requires greater physical interaction as the caregiver must manipulate the person being cared for while changing the incontinence product.

Urinary incontinence (UI) is an elaborate name for the unintentional release of urine, which can affect both men and women. Sometimes it's stress incontinence—a minor leak when you sneeze or laugh too hard, or you may have urge incontinence—the sudden need to urinate without enough time to make it to the bathroom. Other times there's a medical reason behind it. UI can be treated.

In men, incontinence can be brought on by medical conditions like an enlarged prostate, diabetes, and Parkinson's disease. It can be common after some types of prostate surgery, too. Sometimes it can develop for reasons we don't completely understand, like overactive bladder. To get the right treatment, your doctor will need to find the cause of your problem.

Doctors referred to as urogynecologists, or urogyns, receive special training to diagnose and treat women with pelvic floor disorders. Although your primary care physician, OB/GYN, or urologist may have knowledge about these problems, a urogyn offers additional expertise. Talk with your doctor about a referral to a urogyn if you have problems of prolapse, and/or troublesome urinary or fecal incontinence and if you have problems with emptying the bladder or rectum, pelvic pain or bladder pain, and fistulas.

Eyes

Taking care of one's eyes should be of primary concern starting at the beginning of one's life. This includes good nutrition, eye examinations periodically to see if there is a need for eye glasses, doing eye exercises, and getting appropriate rest. Only YOU can tell if your eyes need attention. If your eyes or the eyes of the individual you are caring for need attention it is important that you understand what each specialist does. The following breaks down eye specialists.

Ophthalmologists

Ophthalmologists can prescribe glasses or contact lenses and diagnose and treat diseases like glaucoma. Ophthalmologists differ from optometrists and opticians in their levels of training and in what they can diagnose and treat. As a medical doctor who has completed college and at least eight years of additional medical training, an ophthalmologist is licensed to practice medicine and surgery. An ophthalmologist diagnoses and treats all eye diseases, performs eye surgery, and prescribes and fits eyeglasses and contact lenses to correct vision problems.

While ophthalmologists are trained to care for all eye problems and conditions, some eye M.D.s specialize in a specific area of medical or surgical eye care. This person is called a subspecialist. He or she usually completes one or two years of additional, more in-depth training called a fellowship in one of the main subspecialty areas such as glaucoma, retina, cornea, pediatrics, neurology, and plastic surgery, as well as others.

Optometrist

Optometrists provide primary vision care ranging from sight testing and correction to the diagnosis, treatment, and management of vision changes. An optometrist is not a medical doctor. They are licensed to practice optometry, which primarily involves performing eye exams and vision tests, prescribing and dispensing corrective lenses, detecting certain eye abnormalities, and prescribing medications for certain eye diseases.

Optician

Opticians are technicians trained to design, verify, and fit eyeglass lenses and frames, contact lenses, and other devices to correct eyesight. They rely on prescriptions supplied by ophthalmologists or optometrists, but do not test vision or write prescriptions for visual correction. Opticians are not permitted to diagnose or treat eye diseases.

Dental/Teeth/Gums

Maintaining your teeth is a life-long process. Healthy habits should start early in life and continue throughout.

Being able to properly chew (breakdown the food with our teeth) helps enable us to truly absorb the nutrition out of one's food.

There are several essential dental specialist types, including:

Endodontics

Endodontists address issues involving teeth's dental pulp and nerves. These specialists regularly carry out root canals.

Oral and Maxillofacial Radiology

An oral radiologist looks beneath the surface. Using X-rays, these doctors manage diseases, disorders and damage to teeth and facial bones.

Orthodontics

Orthodontists use a variety of methods to treat the bites of children and adults, focusing on the alignment of the jaw and teeth.

Periodontics

Periodontic dentists focus on the health of the tissues that support and surround teeth, such as the gums. They work to prevent, diagnose, and treat diseases or conditions that affect these areas directly.

Prosthodontics

Dentists who specialize in prosthodontics are concerned with the function, health, and maintenance of biocompatible dental substitutes such as dentures and veneers.

Ears, Nose, Throat

Whatever effects the ears, nose, and throat effects one's general well being. No aspect of these three body parts should be ignored. The following is a clinical explanation of each specialist with the hope of clarifying their interconnectedness.

This group is often lumped together and doctors will study all three. Some of the specialists' names will be repeated and their specialties tend to blur lines and cross over.

Ears

Otolaryngologist

Otolaryngologists diagnose and manage diseases of the ears, nose, sinuses, larynx (voice box), mouth, and throat, as well as structures of the neck and face.

They are trained in both the medical and surgical treatment of hearing loss, ear infections, balance disorders, ear noise (tinnitus), and some cranial nerve disorders. Otolaryngologists also manage congenital (birth) disorders of the outer and inner ear.

Otologist

An otologist is a highly trained physician or surgeon that has special training in how to diagnose and treat illnesses and injuries related to the ears. They usually receive more in-depth education on the physical aspects of the ear and how it works.

Nose
Otolaryngologists

Care of the nasal cavity and sinuses is one of the primary skills of otolaryngologists. Problems in the nasal area include allergies, smell disorders, polyps, and nasal obstruction as a result of a deviated septum. They specialize in Rhinology which are disorders of the nose and sinuses such as sinus disorders, nose bleeds, stuffy nose, loss of smell, polyps, and tumors.

Throat
Otolaryngologists

They specialize in Laryngology which is the study of problems of the throat, including voice and swallowing problems. It aslo includes treating sore throat, hoarseness, swallowing disorder, gastroesophageal reflux disease (GERD), infections, and tumors.

Tongue

Several problems can affect your tongue, such as: pain, sores, swelling, changes in taste, changes in color, or change in texture. These problems often aren't serious. However, sometimes your symptoms might occur due to an underlying condition that requires medical treatment.

You can prevent many tongue problems by practicing good oral hygiene. If you are already experiencing tongue problems, some simple home remedies may help relieve your symptoms.

You should make an appointment to see your doctor for diagnosis and treatment if your symptoms are severe, unexplained, or persists for several days with no signs of improvement.

Appendix D

Logbooks

I place a series of valuable forms and lists into action for my clients as soon as I'm hired. These forms have taken thirty years to perfect, and I'm happy to share them with you now. They are a Daily Visit Form that includes an Emergency Phone Numbers List, Grocery Shopping List, Additional Information Form, and a Medication Chart; and the all-important seven-page Client Information Form. Each is included in this appendix so that you can fill them out. I hope you make them a vital part of your caregiving challenge. Good luck.

Emergency Phone Numbers

I have this list of emergency phone numbers typed and periodically updated, and then printed in a large, readable font. This information is put in a plastic sleeve. A copy is put on the refrigerator, where it can be easily taken down and brought along if a client should need to go into an ambulance or to the hospital. Another copy, also in a plastic sleeve, is placed near every phone. At the top I always include the client's full name, complete address, and phone number. This basic information is first because sometimes when calling 911 or another service, a senior may not remember his own address or phone number.

The emergency phone number list contains the numbers of all contact persons. With the assistance of each family member, I design and print the list in the priority indicated by the following emergency numbers:

Elder Care Made Easier

Daily Visit Form

Name: _____Page: _____

Phone Numbers
- Emergency number _____
- Primary doctor(s) _____
- Ambulance _____
- Hospital of choice _____
- Primary involved family member _____
- Geriatric care manager _____
- Aide and/or care agency _____
- Local senior center_____
- Food delivery service _____
- Transportation service _____

Location:
Home ☐ Hospital ☐ Office ☐ Doctor's office ☐ Other ☐

Contact:
In person ☐ Phone ☐ Letter ☐ Fax ☐ Card ☐ E-mail ☐

General Health:
Excellent ☐ Good ☐ Poor ☐ Frail ☐

Ambulation:
Independent ☐ Cane ☐ Walker ☐ Wheelchair ☐ Bedridden ☐

Appetite:
Excellent ☐ Good ☐ Poor ☐ Eats independently ☐ Must be fed ☐

Bowel and bladder:
Continent ☐ Incontinent of ☐ bowel ☐ bladder ☐ both (B and B)

Cognitive ability:
_____
_____

Communication ability:
Eyes: ☐ Glasses (reading/distance/TV) ☐ Not needed
Hearing: ☐ Hearing aid (right ear/left ear/both) ☐ Not needed
Skin: ☐ Excellent ☐ Breakdown ☐ Location
Sleep: ☐ Full night ☐ Wakes occasionally ☐ Wakes often ☐ Naps ☐ Hardly sleeps ☐ Wanders
Teeth and gums: ☐ Own teeth ☐ Partial dentures ☐ Full dentures ☐ Gums

Problems/concerns:
New medications: (date / /) for _____
Delete medications: (date / /) for _____
Next medical appointment: (date / /) or procedure with:_____

Location_____Phone_____Fax _____

Appendix D

Daily Visit Form (Continued)

Time/Date/Place	Agenda/Activity	Disbursements/Expense/Needs
_____	_____	_____
_____	_____	_____
_____	_____	_____

Grocery Shopping List

Name: _____   Updated __/__/__

The following is an example of a client grocery shopping list. Note that refrigerated and frozen items are the last to be picked up. (Note: These are simply random grocery items taken from a real client's shopping list. I have no loyalty to any particular brand or product.)

Ensure, vanilla

Fruit
Bananas
Grapes
Apples

Vegetables
Carrots and peas
Broccoli and cauliflower
Potatoes and green beans
Bread
Whole wheat bread
English muffins
Canned Foods
Del Monte canned peaches
Bumble Bee tuna
Peanut butter—cream style, no nuts
Palmer All Fruit jelly
Packaged Foods
Spaghetti
Spaghetti sauce
Success rice
Idaho instant mashed potatoes
Bromley tea bags, decaffeinated
Decaffeinated coffee
H-O oatmeal
Desserts
Pound cake
Ice cream—no nuts

Paper Products
Toilet paper
Tissue
Paper towels

Household Products
Ivory Snow washing powder
Dove face soap
Rubber gloves
Brillo pads
Sponges
Ajax
Beverages
Apple juice
Orange juice
Cranberry juice
Condiments, Spices
Mayonnaise
Mustard
Dairy
Milk
Butter
Cream cheese
Swiss cheese
Yogurt
Meat/Fish
Chicken
Turkey
Chopped meat and hamburger patties
Salmon and frozen shrimp

Daily Visit Form (Continued)

Additional Information

Dominant hand: ☐ Right ☐ Left ☐ Ambidextrous
Previous injuries/falls/operations:_____
Scars ☐ Tattoos ☐ Birthmarks ☐ Identifying marks:_____

_____

Number of children: Born _____ Living _____
Birth order of children (with names, nicknames, and married names):

1. _____
2. _____
3. _____
4. _____
5. _____
6. _____
7. _____
8. _____
9. _____
10. _____
11. _____
12. _____
13. _____
14. _____
15. _____

Medications

Pharmacy_____ Address:_____
Phone: _____
Primary doctor:_____ Address: _____
Phone: _____

Medications	Rx #	Doctor	Dosage	Frequency	Diagnosis	Color/size of pill

Daily Visit Form (Continued)

Breakfast	Before Lunch	Lunch	Before Dinner	Dinner	Bedtime

Client Information Form (CIF)

This is my Client Information Form (CIF). I ask the family to fill it out before I meet with their elder so that I have some basic information to work with. It also helps the family determine what they know and don't know about their elder.

Please type or print   Date_____
Patient or Resident
Name:_____Date of birth:_____
                                Age now:_____
Home address: _____ Social Security#_____
Apt. #:_____ Medicare#_____
Medicaid #_____ Chart #_____
Cross streets: _____ Alternate parking:_____
Parking:_____ Restrictions:_____
Travel directions:_____ Hours:_____
Map info:_____ Public transportation:_____
Home phone:_____Business:_____Cell:_____
Fax:_____Beeper:_____E-mail: _____
Does client have (please check all that apply):
☐ Will
☐ Health care proxy
☐ Durable power of attorney (survives incapacity)
☐ DNR (Do Not Resuscitate)
☐ Patient Review Instrument (PRI)
Primary Contact Person
Name: _____ Relationship:_____
Address:_____
Home Phone:_____Business:_____Cell:_____
Home E-mail:_____Business E-mail_____Beeper:_____

Client Information Form (CIF) (Continued)

Billing Person (if different)
Name:_____ Relationship:_____
Address:_____
Home phone:_____Business_____Cell_____

Aide or Nurse   Shift:
Name:_____   Monday:_____
                               Tuesday:_____
Address:_____   Wednesday:_____
_____   Thursday:_____
                               Friday:_____
                               Saturday:_____
                               Sunday:_____
Home phone:_____Business:_____Fax:_____
Cell:_____Beeper:_____E-mail_____
Agency name:_____Fax:_____E-mail_____

Aide or Nurse   Shift:
Name:_____   Monday:_____
                               Tuesday:_____
Address:_____   Wednesday:_____
_____   Thursday:_____
                               Friday:_____
                               Saturday:_____
                               Sunday:_____
Home phone:_____Business:_____Fax:_____
Cell:_____Beeper:_____E-mail_____
Agency name:_____Fax:_____E-mail_____

Doctor   Specialty:_____
Name:_____Emergency phone:_____
                               Hospital phone:_____
Address:_____
Home phone:_____Business:_____Fax:_____
Cell:_____Beeper:_____E-mail_____

Doctor   Specialty:_____
Name:_____Emergency phone:_____
                               Hospital phone:_____
Address:_____
Home phone:_____Business:_____Fax:_____
Cell:_____Beeper:_____E-mail_____

Client Information Form (CIF) (Continued)

Doctor Specialty:_____
Name:_____ Emergency phone:_____
  Hospital phone:_____
Address:_____
Home phone:_____ Business:_____ Fax:_____
Cell:_____ Beeper:_____ E-mail_____

Doctor Specialty:_____
Name:_____ Emergency phone:_____
  Hospital phone:_____
Address:_____
Home phone:_____ Business:_____ Fax:_____
Cell:_____ Beeper:_____ E-mail_____

Dentist Specialty:_____
Name:_____ Emergency phone:_____
  Hospital phone:_____
Address:_____
Home phone:_____ Business:_____ Fax:_____
Cell:_____ Beeper:_____ E-mail_____

Podiatrist Specialty:_____
Name:_____ Emergency phone:_____
  Hospital phone:_____
Address:_____
Home phone:_____ Business:_____ Fax:_____
Cell:_____ Beeper:_____ E-mail_____

Local Pharmacy
Name:_____ Emergency phone:_____
  Hospital phone:_____
Address:_____
Home phone:_____ Business:_____ Fax:_____
Cell:_____ Beeper:_____ E-mail_____

Attorney Specialty:_____
Name:_____ Emergency phone:_____
Address:_____
Home phone:_____ Business:_____ Fax:_____
Cell:_____ Beeper:_____ E-mail_____

Accountant/Financial Advisor Specialty:_____
Name:_____ Emergency phone:_____
Address:_____
Home phone:_____ Business:_____ Fax:_____
Cell:_____ Beeper:_____ E-mail_____

Client Information Form (CIF) (Continued)
Who Has Keys to Patient's Apartment or Home?

Relationship_____
Name:_____Emergency phone:_____
Address:_____
Home phone:_____Business:_____Fax:_____
Cell:_____Beeper:_____E-mail_____

Other Involved Relatives

Relationship_____
Name:_____Emergency phone:_____
Address:_____
Home phone:_____Business:_____Fax:_____
Cell:_____Beeper:_____E-mail_____

Relationship_____
Name:_____Emergency phone:_____
Address:_____
Home phone:_____Business:_____Fax:_____
Cell:_____Beeper:_____E-mail_____

Relationship_____
Name:_____Emergency phone:_____
Address:_____
Home phone:_____Business:_____Fax:_____
Cell:_____Beeper:_____E-mail_____

Neighbors, Doorman, Superintendent, or other Involved Persons

Relationship_____
Name:_____Emergency phone:_____
Address:_____
Home phone:_____Business:_____Fax:_____
Cell:_____Beeper:_____E-mail_____

Relationship_____
Name:_____Emergency phone:_____
Address:_____
Home phone:_____Business:_____Fax:_____
Cell:_____Beeper:_____E-mail_____

Relationship_____
Name:_____Emergency phone:_____
Address:_____
Home phone:_____Business:_____Fax:_____
Cell:_____Beeper:_____E-mail_____

Client Information Form (CIF) (Continued)

Patient Needs

Patient's Medical Condition/Diagnosis:_____

Medications	Dosage	Times	Needed for/Condition

1. _____
2 _____
3. _____
4. _____
5. _____
6. _____
7. _____
8. _____
9. _____
10. _____

Over-the-counter drugs, vitamins, and herbs:_____

Allergies/Allergic to:_____

Additional Information

Languages spoken by patient:_____

Country of birth:_____

Siblings:_____

Mother's maiden name:_____

Mother's full name:_____

Father's full name:_____

U.S. citizen?   Yes ☐   No ☐

Came to this country:_____at age:_____

Car

Is there a car?   Yes ☐   No ☐

Is the client driving?   Yes ☐   No ☐

Who does the driving?_____

Who has the car keys?_____

Organizations

Attends community center, social groups, and volunteers

    Name:_____

    Address:_____

Religious Affiliation

    Now:_____

    Childhood:_____

Client Information Form (CIF) (Continued)

Religious Organizations or Place of Worship:_____

Address:_____

Home phone:_____Business:_____Fax:_____

Cell:_____Beeper:_____E-mail_____

Burial Information

Family name or association:_____

Name:_____Plot number_____

Address:_____

Contact name:_____

Home phone:_____Business:_____Fax:_____

Cell:_____Beeper:_____E-mail_____

Use this space for additional information:_____

_____

_____

_____

_____

_____

_____

_____

_____

_____

_____

_____

_____

_____

_____

Form Completed by:_____

Phone:_____Work:_____

Thank you for taking the time to fill out this Client Information Form (CIF).

www.doctormarion.com

Elder Care A–Z

Caregiving can be an overwhelming challenge. You're not alone. There are millions of others in your position. Make a copy of this list and put it on your refrigerator or desk at work. It could become a shorthand way to keep you organized, and I hope it lifts your spirits.

A Address the issue(s) at hand.

B Be bold and accept the reality of the situation.

C Categorize everything that must be dealt with.

D Delegate where possible.

E Ethical decisions must be made at all times.

F Financial matters should be in order.

G Get going and don't procrastinate.

H Help is available if you search and ask.

I Independence of your elder must be considered at all times.

J Juxtapose your thoughts with your elder's and think about what he or she needs.

K Keep a journal of contacts, including names, dates, times, topics, outcomes, and next steps.

L Legal issues should be handled in a specific and comprehensive manner.

M Make time for your own family, job, and social life.

N Know the desired outcomes, goals, and projected solutions to the challenges.

O Organize your thoughts and plan ways to address each challenge.

P Prioritize your own issues and time constraints.

Q Quality of life, both yours and your elder's, must be addressed.

R Recreation and time away are healthy and necessary for your own peace of mind.

S Search for all resources that might help your caregiving journey.

T Trust the elder you're caring for, and trust your basic caregiving instincts.

U Understand that being a caregiver requires patience.

V Visit your elder in person, or call him or her on the phone, or send cards, letters, flowers, and/or gifts.

W Write out all information and keep it current.

X X-haustion may set in; so find ways to relieve stress.

Y You're doing a great job—congratulate yourself.

Z Zone out and reward yourself for a job well done.

Index